Parent ~~PARTNER~~SHIPS
IN A PLC AT WORK®

Forming and Sustaining
School–Home Relationships
With Families

KYLE PALMER

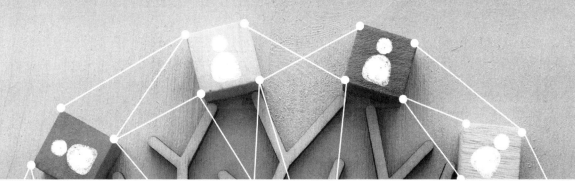

Solution Tree | Press
a division of
Solution Tree

555 North Morton Street
Bloomington, IN 47404
800.733.6786 (toll free) / 812.336.7700
FAX: 812.336.7790

email: info@SolutionTree.com
SolutionTree.com

Visit **go.SolutionTree.com/PLCbooks** to download the free reproducibles in this book.

Printed in the United States of America

Library of Congress Cataloging-in-Publication Data

Names: Palmer, Kyle, author.
Title: Parentships in a PLC at work : forming and sustaining school-home
   relationships with families / Kyle Palmer.
Description: Bloomington, IN : Solution Tree Press, [2022] | Includes
   bibliographical references and index.
Identifiers: LCCN 2022000150 (print) | LCCN 2022000151 (ebook) | ISBN
   9781952812514 (paperback) | ISBN 9781952812521 (ebook)
Subjects: LCSH: Professional learning communities. | Home and school. |
   Education--Parent participation.
Classification: LCC LB1731 .P335 2022 (print) | LCC LB1731 (ebook) | DDC
   371.19/2--dc23/eng/20220212
LC record available at https://lccn.loc.gov/2022000150
LC ebook record available at https://lccn.loc.gov/2022000151

Solution Tree
Jeffrey C. Jones, CEO
Edmund M. Ackerman, President

Solution Tree Press
President and Publisher: Douglas M. Rife
Associate Publisher: Sarah Payne-Mills
Managing Production Editor: Kendra Slayton
Editorial Director: Todd Brakke
Art Director: Rian Anderson
Copy Chief: Jessi Finn
Senior Production Editor: Suzanne Kraszewski
Content Development Specialist: Amy Rubenstein
Acquisitions Editor: Sarah Jubar
Proofreader: Jessi Finn
Associate Editor: Sarah Ludwig
Editorial Assistants: Charlotte Jones and Elijah Oates

Acknowledgments

This book is dedicated to my loving and amazing wife, Tarah, and our four kids, Karson, Klaire, Kal, and Kauffman. Without their unconditional love and support, this book would not have been possible. All of you make me so proud and were a driving force behind the concept of this book.

I also dedicate this book to my parents, Dick and Jo Palmer. They raised my two brothers, my sister, and myself by providing us with everything we needed: a strong work ethic, a sense of humor, and a love for people.

Special thanks to the numerous amazing educators and parents that I have had the opportunity to work with over the years. Through my work as a teacher, principal, human resources director, and consultant, I have learned so much from all of you. The world of education is in good hands with all of your talents and expertise.

Finally, to my many mentors and PLC practitioners who have helped to mold me into the leader I am today, thank you from the bottom of my heart.

Solution Tree Press would like to thank the following reviewers:

Steve Barkley
Education Consultant
PLS 3rd Learning
Basel Area, Switzerland

Joann Calabrese
Adjunct Professor
Indiana University
Bloomington, Indiana

Kevin Carroll
Principal
Sparks High School
Sparks, Nevada

Chad Luhman
Assistant Principal
Lexington Traditional
    Magnet School
Lexington, Kentucky

David Pillar
Assistant Director
Hoosier Hills Career Center
Bloomington, Indiana

Jennifer Steele
Assistant Principal
Northside High School
Fort Smith, Arkansas

Marcia Tate
Educational Consultant
Developing Minds, Inc.
Conyers, Georgia

Visit **go.SolutionTree.com/PLCbooks** to download the free reproducibles in this book.

Table of Contents

Reproducibles are in italics.

About the Author

 **Kyle Palmer, EdD,** is the award-winning former principal of Lewis and Clark Elementary in Liberty, Missouri. Kyle is a passionate believer in the power of professional learning communities (PLCs) and uses his leadership experiences and expertise to help schools build collaborative cultures to implement the right work to improve student learning for all. Kyle is also a passionate believer in identifying and growing leaders to help grow the capacity of the learning organization.

Kyle was named the Distinguished Principal for the Clay-Platte region of the Missouri Association of Elementary School Principals in 2013 and won the New Principal Award from the same region in 2009. Under his leadership, Lewis and Clark was designated as a Model PLC school by Solution Tree, as well as an ICLE Model School in 2015, 2016, and 2017 by the International Center for Leadership in Education. Kyle is also a John Maxwell–trained speaker, trainer, and coach.

He received his bachelor's degree in elementary education from the University of Northern Iowa, his master's degree in education leadership from Drake University, and his doctorate in education leadership from Baker University. Kyle, his wife Tarah, and their four children reside in Liberty, Missouri.

To learn more about Kyle's work, follow him on Twitter @DrKylePalmer and on Instagram (kpalmer4).

To book Kyle Palmer for professional development, contact pd@Solution Tree.com.

Introduction

One of the most fundamental purposes we have as a society is ensuring that every individual receives a rich education. Growing up, people have two very important teachers in their lives: their teachers at home and their teachers at school. Unfortunately, it can be difficult, at times, for schools and families to navigate the dynamic relationship between the two of them. Teachers and parents may have different views on what education looks like for each student. No matter the differences, one thing is true: if students are to master essential learning and life skills, schools and parents must work together.

In the spring of 2019, our three-year-old son Kauffman was struggling mightily with his speech. For a long time, I rationalized his delay in speech, attributing it to his being the youngest of four children. My mother always told me that, as a child, I had started talking late because I, too, was the youngest of four children. As I was always told, it was just hard for the youngest to get a word in with so much else happening in the family.

Kauffman's older siblings did not struggle in school, so deep down, I could not understand why Kauffman was struggling. As time went by, my initial rationalizations began to fade. Thankfully, my wife, who is also a school administrator, knew better and took the appropriate actions, starting by scheduling assessments to determine whether Kauffman might have a disability. In my career as an educator, I sat through a few hundred individual education program (IEP) meetings, but as a parent, I was halfway through my first one. I was confused and frustrated, and I prayed that help would come his way. It took my first meeting as a parent for me to see how important the previous hundreds were.

As an educator, I see daily how important it is for schools and families to work together. I also see how their work together could be so much better and more effective. I knew that for Kauffman to learn and grow, my wife and I would need to work hand in hand with his school. I understood the

Nowhere is the two-way street of learning more in disrepair and in need of social reconstruction than in the relationships among parents, communities, and their schools.

—Michael Fullan

importance of that collaboration and vowed to make that commitment, and I trusted his school to do the same. All students deserve that—what I call a *strong parentship*—a partnership between parents (or other caregivers, such as guardians or grandparents) and their children's schools to better leverage parents' impact on their children's learning. When I refer to a *parentship* or *parent* in this book, I am referring not only to parents but to guardians, grandparents, and all the special adults that may be involved in helping students succeed.

Most would agree that students should always be at the forefront of our focus in education. School leadership expert Tom Hierck describes how "schools exist as learning centers for children, not employment centers for adults" (T. Hierck, personal communication, April 14, 2020). School administrators, teachers, and other educators view school through a lens different from that of parents. Educators constantly think about what program, support, learning, or need is in place for a student and what they are going to do to help. Parents, grandparents, aunts, uncles, and other guardians constantly consider how a child feels about school and if that child is safe and treated fairly. When schools and parents are not on the same page, it can cause tension, anxiety, and stress. The first thing we must do to remedy this disconnect is to admit that it exists and work to have a student view of school. That is, we must always ask, "Are we working together to do what is best for the student?"

Current Reality

The following story that elementary school teacher Julie Marburger posted about on Facebook is a perfect example of what happens when parent-school relationships decay (Lavalle, 2021). Marburger had reached her breaking point in the spring of 2019, making the decision to resign. She cited disrespectful parents, limited resources, fear for her personal safety and the safety of her students, the need to spend her own money on school supplies that would inevitably be destroyed, and the general lack of support from building administration as reasons for her resignation. After one encounter with a parent who blamed her for her son's failures, Julie went to Facebook to vent her frustrations. Her post went viral, and as it garnered more and more attention, other educators commented with descriptions of similar experiences and frustrations over poor school budgets, overbearing parents, and the general stress that is a teacher's everyday life.

Business consultant Jim Collins (2001) describes what he calls *the Stockdale Paradox* in the corporate world: maintaining "an unwavering faith in the endgame" and "a commitment to prevail as a great company despite the brutal facts" (p. 83). With regard to parent-school relations, we must recognize the necessity for strong parental partnership with schools and understand that the existing partnership needs to improve. Unfortunately, those relationships that should be strong are rather frayed and decaying.

Parental involvement is lowest among families who fall below the poverty line or whose children qualify for free or reduced lunch (Child Trends, 2018). This is also true for families who do not speak English or who have limited English proficiency. In addition, low-income African American parents who lack a strong educational background are even more likely to be disconnected from their children's education and often intentionally avoid schools and their teachers (Williams & Sánchez, 2012). Although it's difficult to admit, this is commonly due to teachers' and other school staff's perceptions about these same parents' ability to be active and positively involved in their children's education. This results in a paradox: oftentimes, students who need the most-involved parents have the least-involved parents (Cherry, 2021).

An opportunity gap certainly exists between low-income families and middle- and upper-class families. Families in poverty may not have the financial resources to access the internet and online learning resources. The COVID-19 pandemic exacerbated this discrepancy. Schools turned to online learning, which worked well for the students who had access to online resources, but it further delayed the learning of students who didn't (Carminucci, Hodgman, Rickles, & Garet, 2021).

Higher Ed Dive (2019) reports that of the one thousand primary teachers across the United States who participated in the 2019 *State of Parent Engagement* survey, 55 percent stated that they did not understand the importance of parental involvement in their classroom. In addition, 54 percent believed that education was the teacher's job, not a collaboration between parents and teachers. It may seem noble that these teachers are owning their professional obligations to ensure students learn, but they are really missing the point about how to involve parents in the journey. In fact, parents can and need to be used as a prized and plentiful resource.

Willard Waller was a sociologist and conducted his research primarily on the sociology of the family, education, and the connection between families and education. Waller (1932) made the following observation:

> From the ideal point of view, parents and teachers have much in common, in that both, supposedly, wish things to occur for the best interests of the child; but, in fact, parents and teachers usually live in a condition of mutual distrust and enmity. Both wish the child well, but it is such a different kind of well that conflict must inevitably arise over it. The fact seems to be that parents and teachers are natural enemies, predestined each for the discomfiture of the other. (p. 68)

Even though his comments date back to the early 20th century, we sadly see this still playing out in our 21st century schools.

A Golden Opportunity

Earlier in this introduction, I referenced Collins's Stockdale Paradox, whose critical component is that we must believe to our core that we can achieve excellence. We will do so by confronting the brutal facts, getting an accurate view of our current state of affairs to truly fix what has been broken. In terms of parent-school partnerships, it is time to build a stronger bridge and learn how everyone can collaborate for students' benefit.

According to researchers Charles Fadel, Maya Bialik, and Bernie Trilling (2015), electing not to change the current education system is itself a choice or an action—and one that will only perpetuate existing problems. Educators are a resilient and hardworking group able to rally together to face new initiatives, laws, and obstacles. Building school-home partnerships is no different; with intentional thought and planning, educators can nurture positive, productive school-home partnerships. The rest of this book will lay out how to achieve this.

About This Book

My hope is that after reading this book, every preK–12 teacher, counselor, social worker, and principal has the tools and skills necessary to partner with parents to ensure all students learn at high levels. Specifically, this book will be a resource for those schools undergoing professional learning community (PLC) transformation, serving to improve staff's means of connecting with parents so they can expand parental involvement and further the school's work. Including parents in a much deeper level of collaboration will help to increase student learning and contribute to what Richard DuFour, Rebecca DuFour, Robert Eaker, Thomas W. Many, and Mike Mattos (2016) call "the right work" you need to focus on in your PLC (p. 12). As collaborative teams in your PLC develop more urgency to take collective responsibility and adopt an action orientation toward increased performance for all students, they can look to this book to find effective, evidence-based ideas to implement in their own work.

As you already know, being a PLC is very different from being a traditional school. When schools and districts commit to align to the PLC process, they are committing to a laser-like focus on student learning in a results-driven collaborative culture. Improving your parentships will allow you to work more closely with parents, inviting them to become partners and to support the focus on student learning in this collaborative culture. Traditional schools say they want to better collaborate with parents; PLCs actually do it by developing strong parentships.

The book explores parentships in two parts: (1) foundations of parentships in a PLC and (2) strategies for parentships in a PLC.

Part 1: Foundations of Parentships in a PLC

Part 1 provides the foundational information on parentships, identifying what they are and how to create them. Chapter 1 defines a *parentship* and outlines the shifts that must occur in a PLC as the school engages more fully with the parent community. It reviews the three big ideas and four critical questions of a PLC (DuFour et al., 2016)—the fundamental elements of a PLC—and then situates those elements within a parentship to show how parentships enhance the traditional PLC process. Chapter 2 illustrates the benefits of strong parentships in a PLC and how to create those parentships by first establishing a parentship success team. Chapter 3 outlines why parentship mission and vision statements are important and how, through intentionally involving parents in collaboration to support students, they build on PLC mission and vision statements. The chapter also provides a process for writing mission and vision statements. Chapter 4 explores why parentship values and goals are important and how they build on PLCs' use of values, or collective commitments, and goals to ignite stronger educator and parent collaboration. The chapter also provides a process for writing collective commitments and goals to monitor successful implementation of parentships at your school.

Part 2: Strategies for Parentships in a PLC

The chapters in part 2 detail how to build parentships using schoolwide strategies, as well as strategies that educators can implement in the classroom. Chapter 5 explores strategies related to curriculum, and chapter 6 provides strategies related to individual student progress. Chapter 7 offers specific ways to increase parental engagement, and chapter 8 covers different methods for reaching out to parents. Finally, chapter 9 presents strategies that can help you monitor and sustain your focus on implementing strong parentships.

The chapters in part 2 contain descriptive Think, Plan, and Act sections to help you and your school develop and plan an action orientation toward implementing the strategies each chapter explores to improve your own parentships. For each one, you will pick a strategy, identify who is responsible to lead the strategy, determine essential resources, list specific action steps needed to successfully implement the strategy, think about something you can stop doing to ensure you have the time to properly focus on this new implementation, and establish how you will follow up on the success of the strategy by scanning for signs that indicate whether the strategy is helping.

Pause and Ponder

Throughout parts 1 and 2, you will find opportunities to stop and reflect on the current reality of parent partnerships in your building or district. These Pause and Ponder reflections push you to think more deeply about how to take meaningful actions to plan next steps to improve the parent partnerships in your PLC.

Long-Lasting Partnerships

It is my hope that this book will provide you and your colleagues with clear steps to get started to build long-lasting school-home partnerships. Let's get started!

Part 1
FOUNDATIONS OF PARENTSHIPS IN A PLC

The chapters in part 1 of this book provide the foundation for how to build strong parentships in your school and district. They provide greater detail on what exactly a parentship is, the three big ideas in a parentship, and the four critical questions to reflect upon as you build your parentship initiative. Part 1 also highlights what the many benefits of parentships are as well as how you will leverage a shared mission, vision, collective commitments, and goals to create and establish your own parentship initiative.

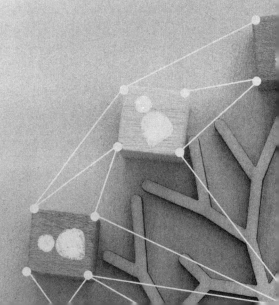

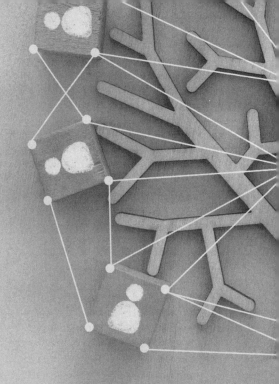

1

Understanding Parentships in a PLC

This chapter will establish a deeper understanding of parentships and their importance in your PLC to help you and your colleagues better improve student learning. This chapter provides clarity on the PLC process to ensure everyone has a common understanding of the core components. This foundation is then extended to connect to how parentships can help to support parents in the PLC process. We'll explore the three big ideas of a parentship, as well as the four critical questions of a parentship in a PLC, before analyzing the shifts in a PLC that your school must go through to more fully develop your parentships.

Creating a strong partnership with parents and families is certainly aligned with the assumptions and practices inherent in professional learning communities.

—Rick DuFour, Rebecca DuFour, and Robert Eaker

Parentships Defined

If you have been thinking that *parentship* is a made-up word, you would be right! *Parentship* is the state of having a trusting and robust collaboration between parents and educators, with an intentional focus on student growth. In a PLC, parentships better leverage parents' impact on their children's learning in the collaborative culture by equipping parents with the tools necessary for them, along with the school, to make a positive impact on their children's learning. Parentships are a more specific way to focus on the dynamic, powerful partnership between parents and educators that is critical to student success. Parentships include a student's parent, guardian, or caregiver or another adult who is working to help improve the student's success in school and life.

Involvement Versus Engagement

Before we go much further, it is important to make the distinction between *parental involvement* and *parental engagement* and understand how they differ, as both are needed in schools.

Parental involvement is often the first step toward deeper parental engagement. When schools ask parents to attend school events, such as concerts, carnival nights, and art shows, the schools are asking parents to be involved—to be present. In these examples, parents are involved but not necessarily engaged. When parents are engaged, they have voices and are listened to. Eliciting parental engagement is more than inviting parents to be present; it's asking parents for their thoughts and feedback about the school. Table 1.1 highlights the differences between parental involvement and parental engagement. The goal in a parentship should be full engagement.

Table 1.1: Parental Involvement Versus Parental Engagement

Parental Involvement	Parental Engagement
Teacher sets student learning goals for parents to review	Teachers, parents, and students collaboratively set student learning goals
Student may or may not develop a desire to learn without support from parents and educators collaborating	Student develops a desire to be a lifelong learner with support from educators and parents
School tells parents	School talks with parents
Teacher stands in front of parent	Teacher and parent sit side by side
Parent attends school activities	Parent helps plan school activities
School leads with its mouth	School leads with its ears
Teachers find out information about students from school experiences	Parents provide teachers with important information on students
School is an adviser	Parent is a partner
School provides parent with information	School asks parents for their feedback
Partnership is solid	Partnership is rock solid

Pause and Ponder

What is the critical difference between parental involvement and parental engagement? Consider some ways your school currently involves parents and engages parents.

The PLC Process

For schools and students to be successful, numerous variables must be in place. Educators need to focus on teaching fewer standards. Educators also need to establish and work within a collaborative culture where all educators work toward the success of all students, not just the students in their own classrooms. Educators must also have a process for establishing and monitoring goals so they know if students are learning. All of these variables are inherent in the PLC at Work process. Since the early 1990s, the PLC at Work process has emerged to provide a framework for continuous improvement all educators can implement to create the structures necessary to improve student learning. A *PLC* is "an ongoing process in which educators work collaboratively in recurring cycles of collective inquiry and action research to achieve better results for the students they serve" (DuFour et al., 2016, p. 10). The PLC process includes the foundational elements of three big ideas and four critical questions that guide the work of teams (DuFour et al., 2016).

The Three Big Ideas in a PLC

PLCs are laser focused on three big ideas: (1) a focus on learning, (2) a collaborative culture and collective responsibility, and (3) a results orientation (DuFour et al., 2016). In a PLC, educators commit to one another to work in collaborative teams in a cycle of collective inquiry focused on results to ensure all students learn at high levels.

A Focus on Learning

When a school or district functions as a PLC, educators commit to insisting on high levels of learning for all students as the reason the school exists and their fundamental responsibility as educators. To achieve this purpose, educators within a PLC do the following:

> Create and are guided by a clear and compelling vision of what the organization must become in order to help all students learn. They make collective commitments clarifying what each member will do to create such an organization, and they use results-oriented goals to mark their progress. Members work together to clarify exactly what each student must learn, monitor each student's learning on a timely basis, provide systematic interventions that ensure students receive additional time and support for learning when they struggle, and extend their learning when students have already mastered the intended outcomes. (DuFour et al., 2016, p. 11)

To do this, teams within a PLC must measure every action—every practice and process—and challenge those actions that don't measure up in order to align to the purpose of learning for all.

A Collaborative Culture and Collective Responsibility

The second big idea, a collaborative culture and collective responsibility, means that "to ensure all students learn at high levels, educators must work collaboratively and take collective responsibility for the success of each student" (DuFour et al., 2016, p. 12).

In a PLC, collaboration is not optional—it is expected. Therefore, educators in a PLC work *interdependently* as members of collaborative teams to achieve *common goals* for which members are *mutually accountable* (DuFour et al., 2016). The common goals schools and teams create are directly linked to the purpose of learning for all. Schools cannot achieve the fundamental purpose of learning if teachers work in isolation.

As author and motivational speaker Simon Sinek (2012) notes about collaborative teams, "A team is not a group of people who work together. A team is a group of people who trust each other." Author and lecturer Brené Brown (2018b) describes collaboration as being tough. It takes rumbling, circling back, and constantly staying brave in the face of the hard work of collaboration. "And," she adds, staying brave "produces something far more powerful than you could ever do alone" (Brown, 2018b).

A Results Orientation

The third big idea in a PLC is a results orientation. PLCs focus on results by assessing and monitoring student achievement to see whether students are learning, and then they "use that evidence of learning to inform and improve their professional practice and respond to individual students who need intervention or enrichment" (DuFour et al., 2016, p. 12). Members of PLCs do not just hope that what teams and individual teachers are doing is working; hope is not a strategy for success. Rather, PLCs implement data-driven decision making as a high-leverage action to monitor learning. The evidence PLCs use is relevant to what students should understand and know how to do. These data provide evidence of student achievement, as well as feedback on the effectiveness of teacher practices.

The three big ideas of a PLC provide a strong foundation for schools to think through and reflect on as they work to implement a deeply engrained PLC culture. To support you and your teams in building parentships, I have drawn a parallel to the three big ideas of a PLC with the three big ideas in a parentship. The three big ideas of a parentship provide guidance for how PLCs can involve parents and guardians in the work of their PLC.

The Three Big Ideas in a Parentship

In the following sections, we will consider the three big ideas as they apply to creating and implementing parentships.

A Focus on Parent Learning

As you know, the first big idea in a PLC is to ensure all students learn at high levels. In parentships, you must make sure all *parents* also are learning. Caregivers need to learn how to best support students at home and better understand teachers' expectations for students' learning and skill development. Most parents lack an education background and consequently aren't sure how to provide support at home. Sometimes parents are even intimidated by schoolwork and school personnel. Increasing parent learning will help to increase student learning.

Pause and Ponder

In what ways do you currently focus on increasing the learning in your parent community? What are some ways you can do this better in the future?

A Collaborative Culture and Collective Responsibility

The second big idea in a PLC, a collaborative culture and collective responsibility, is also important for parentships. The PLC process typically centers on students and educators. Expanding the focus on collaborative culture and collective responsibility beyond the school building to parents and other caregivers allows them to be involved and engaged in the education process—to actively understand and participate in students' education. Adding parents creates an education triangle. The area in the middle, where they all intersect, is the goal, a focus on learning.

Peter Coleman (1998) in his study of schools identifies what he calls *the power of three*: parent, student, and teacher collaboration. Coleman (1998) argues that "student commitment to schooling (or engagement in learning) is primarily shaped by parents through the 'curriculum of the home'; but this parent involvement is an alterable variable which can be influenced by school and teacher practices" (p. 11).

Schools traditionally focus their work on what educators in the building are going to do to ensure success for each student. While doing so, they get caught up in meeting so many various demands that they often forget about the crucial third piece to educational success for all students: parents and the home.

With intention and a proactive approach, schools can involve parents in ways that are beneficial to the learning process. In *Revisiting Professional Learning Communities at Work: New Insights for Improving Schools*, Richard DuFour, Rebecca DuFour, and Robert Eaker (2008) clarify this idea by stating that:

> If uninformed people are asked to make decisions, they will make uninformed decisions. If educators are to engage parents in significant decisions, they must include them in the process to build shared knowledge of the current reality and best practice. If this crucial step is ignored, parent participation in governance and decision-making can do more harm than good. (p. 390)

When parents are more actively involved in the PLC process, you complete the educational triangle among students, teachers, and parents. Author and educational consultant Michael Fullan (2010a) describes this powerful connection:

> The power of collective capacity is that it enables ordinary people to accomplish extraordinary things—for two reasons. One is that knowledge about effective practice becomes more widely available and accessible on a daily basis. The second reason is more powerful still—working together generates commitment. Moral purpose, when it stares you in the face through students and your peers working together to make lives and society better, is palpable, indeed virtually irresistible. The collective motivational well seems bottomless. (p. 72)

Facilitating Two-Way Communication

There are several strategies you can use to help you establish an education triangle. First, build relationships through two-way communication. In education, we talk about the importance of relationships between teachers and students. For obvious reasons, these are critically important relationships, but school staff must also excel in relationships with parents and guardians. Relationship building is primarily the responsibility of the educator, not the parent. To have strong relationships, you must be open, honest, and intentional.

It is important to note that I am not advocating for *more* communication; rather, I am advocating for *better* communication. Lengthy newsletters often go home with students only to remain unread in the bottom of backpacks or in piles of papers on the dining room table. Busy families simply do not have the time to look through lengthy documents. Schools must focus on sharing the important news as quickly as possible. Keeping messages short and sweet gets the point across. Teachers can also direct parents to their classroom or school website.

Having strong relationships with caregivers requires educators to have influence on them as well. Having influence is not always easy. In all interactions, educators must continually think about how to increase their influence. For example, teachers might react defensively when parents inquire about teaching practices they have been using for decades, when in fact parents may be asking not because they oppose the strategies but because they simply don't understand them. This defensiveness will come across negatively to parents. When the educators come across this way, they are not able to build influence. When someone has influence with others, that person has the capacity to inform their character, development, or behavior, and decisions are easier to understand. When an educator has influence with a parent, the parent will be more comfortable asking questions of and providing feedback to the teacher.

Listening

The second thing you can do to help establish an education triangle is to be a good listener. Often, when people say they are listening, what they are doing is thinking about what their response is going to be. As writer Caren Osten (2016) explains:

> Research shows that only about 10 percent of us listen effectively. . . . We often *think* that we are listening but we're actually just considering how to jump in to tell our own story, offer advice, or even make a judgment—in other words, we are not listening to *understand*, but rather to *reply*.

Teachers must ask themselves, "Am I truly engaging parents and valuing their feedback? Or am I just trying to get my point across?" This is great reflective thinking and important in this process so teachers are sure they are truly listening. Involving parents means inviting them to events at the school. Engaging parents means asking them thoughtful questions to elicit feedback. As Fullan (2016) concludes, "Schools do not capitalize enough on the interest in and knowledge of their own children's learning that many parents have" (p. 174). Parents may feel removed from or even skeptical of their child's education, but when parents are truly engaged and the school reaches out to them in a meaningful way, parents will be more likely to become engaged and thus share invaluable insights about their child.

Understanding Perspective

The third thing you can do to establish the education triangle is to understand proper perspective. There are two ways most people see the world. The first is through their own lens, what I call the *primary perspective*. The second way is through someone else's lens, or the *secondary perspective*. Most people use the primary perspective, seeing the world as it affects them, not how it affects others. In a *Harvard Business Review* article, researcher Francesca Gino (2019) concludes, "The task for leaders is to encourage an outward focus in everyone, challenging the tendency we all have to fixate on ourselves—what we'd like to say and achieve—instead of what we can learn from others" (p. 75). For example, a teacher may see a need to create a behavior plan for a student because the student's actions are impacting the teacher's ability to teach (primary perspective). The teacher would be wise to consider a secondary perspective by thinking about the student's motivations for acting out. Does the teacher need to build a relationship with the student so they don't act out so much in class? The student's parents might see the situation through another lens—they might believe another student is impacting their child's behavior in class.

Pause and Ponder

Does your school truly believe in and understand the education triangle? What strategies can you use to build your education triangle?

It is human nature for people to see the world through the primary perspective. Marianna Pogosyan (2019) calls this idea *motivated perception*, the idea that people see the world in a biased, selective, and malleable way to benefit themselves. Thus, they make decisions based on how they themselves will be impacted. Schools are no different because schools consist of, well, people.

To engage parents in student learning, educators must learn to adopt the secondary perspective, taking a step back to consider how planning and decision making will impact parents and to intentionally include them in those processes. Table 1.2 highlights what intentionally engaging with parents might look like through the primary perspective and the secondary perspective.

Table 1.2: Primary Versus Secondary Perspective

Primary Perspective	Secondary Perspective
Our school mission statement is as follows.	What are your thoughts on our school mission statement?
We will hold parent-teacher conferences the same way we did last year—in the evenings only.	Based on parent feedback, we are going to offer some early-afternoon time this year for parent-teacher conferences.
I sent home some work for Annelise to complete there. Could you please do it with her?	What resources do you need at home to help Annelise? I will send some home and then call you to explain it all.
Parents, could you please email me your questions or concerns?	Parents, please call me whenever you have a question or concern. I always have time for you.
If you were doing more with your child at home, he wouldn't be so far behind.	I will do all I can to make sure your child is not so far behind.

Handling Conflict Appropriately

The final element of establishing the education triangle is handling conflict appropriately. There are always going to be problems; this can't be changed. Parents will want to protect students, and teachers will be inclined to protect their teaching philosophies and strategies, as well as students. How best to support the students is the primary source of conflict. It's not the conflict that destroys relationships; it's the poor handling of conflict that destroys them.

Pause and Ponder

How do you best deal with conflict between yourself and parents? What strategies do you use or can you use to turn conflict into effective problem solving?

There must be a process that lays out ground rules for addressing conflict. The following process can help teachers and parents work together and move forward to resolve the conflict.

1. **Listen to understand:** When conflict arises, people often become defensive and raise their voices to be heard. When you listen to understand, you are careful not to become defensive, and you don't take high tempers of others too personally. It will help in the end to allow someone to blow off some steam and feel better about being heard. After a short period of blowing off steam, the conversation should become much more respectful.

   For example, a parent calls you on the phone and immediately begins to raise their voice because they are frustrated that their child received a C on their last test. The parent is angry because they believe it wasn't fair for their child to get a C because the test was unannounced and the parent believes that you didn't spend enough time in class to learn the objectives being assessed on the test. At this point, the best thing to do is listen and allow the parent to vent. You do so, and after a few minutes the parent begins to calm down.

   By no means should any educator have to take continued disrespect and elongated periods of yelling or screaming. Being threatened is never OK, and other actions are necessary when an educator feels threatened, such as communicating the threatening situation to the appropriate school administrators.

2. **List information:** Oftentimes, conflict arises from misunderstandings. Take out the emotion and describe what is

factually correct and what is false information. To continue the example from item one, after the parent begins to calm down and lower their voice, this is the time where you can change the trajectory. Lay out factual information about the situation. State that the test was indeed announced and posted on the class website for the past week, you emailed reminders, and the students worked on the content to be tested during the previous five days in class. The final point you can make is that you allowed the student to retake the test and the student declined.

3. **Brainstorm possible solutions:** When all relevant information is known, shift the focus to the future by problem solving. Brainstorm all possible solutions without trying to limit your ideas. After you list the factual information, provide the parent with an opportunity to respond. In the example, you are effectively handling the conflict. The parent responds by acknowledging they did not know the test was indeed announced one week earlier and their child had not informed them that retakes had been offered. You can then jump in to provide possible solutions, such as the opportunity to retake the test after reviewing notes from class that cover the learning objectives to be tested. You even offer additional intervention times with the student to again cover the new learning. The parent states they can cover the material at home with the student and quiz them about the learning.

4. **Decide on the best way to move forward:** Mutually agree on the best solutions you brainstormed together. In the example, both you and the parent agree on a plan to move forward that involves the student working with the parent to review the material at home and then retaking the test.

5. **Follow up:** Follow up one week later to ensure mutual accountability. One week later, the student retook the test and got an A. This is an example of a win-win situation. The student learned the essential standards and the parent and educator resolved a conflict in a very productive and positive way.

A Focus on Results With Parents

You must also apply the third big idea in a PLC—a focus on results—to parentships. Good intentions are, well, just good intentions. Your PLC must look at data to ensure parents are learning and, ultimately, students are learning. Analyzing parents' feedback following their involvement and engagement, as well as their attendance at key school functions, such as parent-teacher conferences and parent nights, will help you monitor their learning.

Goals should be written to be able to monitor results about parent and student learning by using the following SMART-R acronym.

- **S:** Strategic and specific
- **M:** Measurable
- **A:** Attainable
- **R:** Results oriented
- **T:** Time bound
- **R:** Reinforced

The Four Critical Questions of a PLC

Schools and collaborative teacher teams committed to the PLC process focus their work around four critical questions:

1. What knowledge, skills, and dispositions should every student acquire as a result of this unit, this course, or this grade level?

2. How will we know when each student has acquired the essential knowledge and skills?

3. How will we respond when some students do not learn?

4. How will we extend the learning for students who are already proficient? (DuFour et al., 2016, p. 36)

When collaborative teams focus their work on these four questions, they are fixated on the right work in a PLC. Creating a deep understanding of the right work around these four questions allows the school to stay laser focused on student achievement.

The right work teams do to answer these four questions includes defining essential learning outcomes, consistently analyzing student work, implementing common formative assessments, analyzing the results of these assessments, designing a system of interventions and supports for struggling students, extending the work for proficient students, and developing a culture of celebration. While the four questions help collaborative teams carry out this type of work, they can also help PLCs develop their parentships.

The Four Critical Parentship Questions

The following four critical questions will help you shift your attention to parent learning and strongly commit to parentships in your PLC.

1. What do parents need to know and be able to do to support student learning?

2. How will we know parents understand how to help student learning?

3. What will we do to support parents who aren't equipped to help student learning?

4. What will we do to support parents in extending students' learning?

Answering these four critical questions will allow members of a PLC to thoughtfully plan for and advance parents' and caregivers' learning and determine how they will respond if there is no evidence of learning. Parents are a valuable resource in the educational process. As you work toward increased levels of student learning, address these parentship questions in sequential order to focus the conversation around partnering with parents.

Pause and Ponder

Why are the four critical parentship questions so important? How can you help to communicate these to the rest of your PLC?

Necessary Shifts for a Parentship

For your PLC to deeply embrace parentships and arrange for intentional collaboration and engagement with parents, certain cultural shifts must occur. Table 1.3 describes the shifts necessary for your PLC to evolve to build parentships.

Table 1.3: Parentship Shifts

Traditional School	PLC	Parentship
From a focus on teaching . . .	to a focus on learning for teachers . . .	to a focus on learning for parents and teachers
From an emphasis on what was taught . . .	to a fixation on what students learn . . .	to a fixation on what students learn and what parents understand students' level of learning to be
From providing individual teachers with curriculum documents such as state standards and curriculum guides . . .	to engaging in collaboration among teachers to focus on the right work of a PLC . . .	to engaging in collaboration among teachers and parents to focus on the right work of a PLC

From invitational support outside of the school day . . .	to directed (that is, required) support occurring during the school day . . .	to directed support occurring during the school day, as well as from parents at home, with assistance from school staff
From individual teachers attempting to discover ways to improve results . . .	to collaborative teams of teachers helping one another to improve . . .	to collaborative teams of teachers and parents helping one another to improve
From "collaboration lite" on matters unrelated to student achievement . . .	to collaboration explicitly focused on issues and questions that most impact student achievement . . .	to collaboration explicitly focused on issues and questions from school and home that most impact student achievement
From decisions made on the basis of individual preferences . . .	to decisions made collectively by building shared knowledge of best practice . . .	to decisions made collectively by building shared knowledge of best practice and parent feedback about students' learning
From independence . . .	to interdependence among school staff . . .	to interdependence among school staff and with the parent community
From the expectation that learning occurs infrequently (on the few days devoted to professional development) . . .	to the expectation that learning is ongoing and occurs as part of routine work practice . . .	to an expectation that learning is ongoing and occurs as part of routine work practice at school and at home
From learning by listening . . .	to learning by doing . . .	to learning from listening to parents and doing what is best for all students

Source: Adapted from DuFour et al., 2016.

Pause and Ponder

What are your thoughts about the differences between a traditional school and a PLC with parentships? How can you help bring clarity to others?

Conclusion

This chapter described in detail components that will help you focus your work to better engage parents and utilize their skills and talents to support all students. It starts with a strong PLC foundation; it ends with a more involved parent community. The next chapter explores how extending your strong PLC foundation to more intentionally engage parents in the learning process will enhance student learning and how you can begin to create parentships in your PLC.

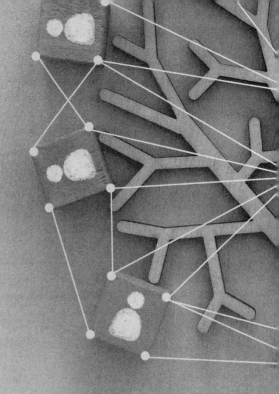

2

Creating Parentships in a PLC

In this chapter, we will look at how you can begin to create parentships in your school. We will discuss the benefits of strong parentships to provide the *why* of parentships. We will then look at *how* to build parentships utilizing a parentship success team. We will explore the similarities and differences between involvement and engagement and take a look at empathy and its role in developing strong parentships.

If you build it, they will come.

—Ray Kinsella
(Kevin Costner),
Field of Dreams

Benefits of Strong Parentships

As Fullan (2016) states, "Parents and other community members are crucial and largely untapped resources who have (or can be helped to have) assets and expertise that are essential to the partnership. . . . Parents are their children's very first educators" (p. 159). There are many benefits of having strong parentships in your school.

Increased Trust

Strong parentships will lead to increased levels of trust. Trust between parents and educators is an essential dynamic for student success. In Stephen M. R. Covey's (2006) ground-breaking research in his best-selling book *The Speed of Trust*, Covey presents his case on the benefit of trust. Covey states that we can increase trust much faster than we think and "doing so will have a huge impact both in the quality of our lives and in the results we're able to achieve" (p. 3). If a parent feels that a teacher has good intentions and is working hard toward the student's success, that same parent will have more reason to trust the teacher. When educators feel parents are doing all they can to support students at home, those educators will be able to build on those relationships for more collaboration geared toward increased student learning. As Brown (2018a) describes, trust is not earned through heroic events or deeds or even highly visible actions; rather, trust is earned by paying attention, listening, and making gestures that convey genuine care and connection. When high levels of trust characterize a relationship, it is easier for both parties to assume the best in each other. Parents will have a more positive view of school and will feel more welcome in the school environment.

Improved Collaboration

Strong parentships will also lead to improved collaboration. Once you establish positive interactions and trust between home and school, you will greatly enhance communication, which can ultimately enable parents and teachers to work together when a student needs more support.

Pause and Ponder

What are some positive and negative elements of your current relationship with parents? What elements would you like to change, if any, and how would you do that?

Improved Student Learning

Finally, there is little doubt that stronger guardian and community participation correlates with higher student success in schools, whether preschool, elementary school, or secondary school. Parental involvement matters, and it matters significantly.

As the Early Learning Network (as cited in Sheridan, 2018) notes in its research findings, "Positive connections between parents and teachers have been shown to improve children's academic achievement, social competencies and emotional well-being. When parents and teachers work as partners, children do better in school and at home." The research study also shows that when educators and parents maintain strong relationships, students' work habits, attitudes about school, and grades improve. Writer Grace Chen (2021) notes that strong parental involvement results in increased academic achievement and improved classroom behavior among students and that families' reading at home can significantly enhance students' reading skills.

According to researcher Elaine M. Allensworth and colleagues (2018), parental engagement has numerous positive impacts:

> There is significant evidence that strong parent engagement practices are related to student achievement. Students who have involved parents are more likely to earn higher grades and test scores, and enroll in higher-level classes; be promoted to the next grade level, pass their classes, and earn more credits; and attend school regularly. Student achievement tends to be higher in schools where principals and teachers are open to parent engagement and view parents as partners in the learning process. Further, there is a substantial body of evidence that parental involvement influences the development of academic mindsets across multiple dimensions. (p. 21)

Lowers Crime and Disorder

Allensworth and colleagues (2018) go on to describe research in Chicago that found that among schools that served students from similar neighborhoods—with similar levels of poverty and similar levels of neighborhood crime—those that had strong relationships between teachers and families had much safer school climates, with lower reports of crime and disorder. Safer school climates promote an environment of learning that supports increased levels of student learning.

Combats Socioeconomic Challenges

The idea that a student's socioeconomic status is the student's biggest indicator of future success is a myth. In his book *Engaging Students With Poverty in Mind*, Eric Jensen (2013) contends that parent education and empowerment are foundational elements of combating the negative effects of socioeconomic challenges. He goes on to state that schools and educators who provide support to parents and families in their homes and build stronger relationships with parents have a high correlation of improved student outcomes.

Increases Student Attendance at School

One major reason student achievement increases with strong parental engagement is because the student is at school more. Students who are in school are going to naturally learn more merely by being present and working with trained professionals. According to a 2015 study by the U.S. Department of Education (2019), more than seven million students missed fifteen or more days of school in 2015–2016. That is 16 percent of the population, or one in every six students. According to the National Survey of Public Education's Response to COVID-19 (Carminucci et al., 2021), student attendance and enrollment during the worldwide pandemic declined in most all cases.

Findings from this study suggest attendance rates declined more significantly in districts that provided less in-person instruction as well as in districts that are high poverty and serve mostly students of color.

Compared to their White peers, American Indian and Pacific Islander students are more than 50 percent more likely to lose three weeks of school or more, Black students 40 percent more likely, and Hispanic students 17 percent more likely (U.S. Department of Education, 2019).

Pause and Ponder

Have you seen evidence of these research findings in your current job or role? How does this research impact your understanding of parental engagement in schools?

How to Build a Parentship

The best way to begin building your parentships is to create a guiding coalition of key members of your school staff, along with key members of your parent and guardian community. This team will then lead the collaborative work needed to establish your own parentships. This guiding coalition team is called the *parentship success team*, or PST.

The PST will become one of the most important leadership teams in your school. In addition to school staff, the PST should include parents who represent various grade levels and departments in the building. For example, the PST in a high school will include parents whose students are in algebra classes, world history classes, literature classes, and so on. The PST in an elementary school will include parents of first graders, parents of second graders, and so on. One parent should be selected to serve as a co-chair with the building principal. The PST members should be a diverse group that represents the ethnic and socioeconomic backgrounds of the students and families who attend your school. Ten to twelve total members is optimal, but fewer or more members might work best for your school community. Half the members should be school staff, with the other half from the parent community. You may also consider aligning with an existing parent group in your building such as a PTO or PTA. If your school has already established a parent group, you may consider forming a committee of parents who will become a part of the PST or modifying your current group to include the diversity needed within your PST. If your building has not yet set up a parent group, follow the steps in this chapter to create your PST.

It is vital to recruit the right people for your PST. Communicate to your parent community your plan, and ask for volunteers. Interview interested parents using the criteria previously described, and make your final selections after you conduct those interviews. Interview questions should also focus on interested parents' availability, commitment to your school, and ability to research and understand decisions that need to be made to improve student learning. When selecting team members, look for the best fit based on their responses to all these types of questions and remember to prioritize the diversity of the team. You can use the same volunteer process for school staff, but make sure at least one of the school team members also sits on the guiding coalition so there is a connection between the work of the PST and the guiding coalition. All the parents on the team should have a student who currently attends the school, and all team members should commit to attending at least 90 percent of the monthly meetings. Meetings should be forty-five to sixty minutes long and can be done in person or virtually. Hold meetings consistently and make them easy for members to attend.

The essential functions of the PST include the following.

- Meet monthly following an established agenda that builds on work from the previous month and includes celebration of accomplishments.

- Create the mission, vision, values (collective commitments), and goals for the school's parentships.

- Begin each meeting with reflection on these core statements by having team members share what they have seen or heard in the past month that reinforces actions aligned to the shared mission and vision.

- Consistently discuss collective team commitments by focusing on one value per meeting throughout the year and how the school community has demonstrated this value.

- Review progress on the parentship goals. Share results from the following surveys (these tools are discussed in detail in chapter 9, page 97):
  - Parentship mission statement continuum (Use each spring as a reflective exercise to guide mission work.)
  - Parentship vision statement continuum (Use each spring as a reflective exercise to guide vision work.)
  - Parentship mission and vision survey (Share results with the parentship advocacy council in spring.)

        □ Parentship-perception survey (Use each spring as a reflective exercise to guide collective commitments.)

        □ Data on student attendance

        □ Student achievement on accountable testing measures

        □ Data on parent attendance at school events

- Advocate for all students, not just their own.

- Serve as a PTA, PTO, and so on (meaning the coalitions should join together as one).

- Discuss common obstacles and barriers that reduce parent and family engagement in the school, and share with school leadership. Brainstorm to collaboratively find ways to address concerns. Parent members should feel comfortable offering ideas for resolution to common barriers.

- School staff on the PST consistently report information from the school's guiding coalition that relates back to student learning and other school events.

Pause and Ponder

There are many advantages to creating a PST. Reflect on any barriers or challenges. What are they, and how could you overcome these?

Use figure 2.1 to organize the essential work of the PST. Items on this sample agenda, such as shared mission, shared vision, values (collective commitments), and goals, are explored in more detail in chapters 3 (page 33) and 4 (page 43). Use figure 2.2 for clarity on who should be added to the PST. After the team is put together, it will be important to select a parent co-chair as well as a school co-chair. The individuals in these roles will be responsible for planning the agenda, overseeing the work, and communicating with each other on that planning. Typically the school co-chair is a principal or an assistant principal, but that is not required.

Empathy

Educators must have the correct mindset to undertake the work of building strong parentships in their schools. The correct mindset begins with educators having empathy for parents, caregivers, and families. Having this empathy allows educators to appreciate what parents want and what they are able to add to the partnership. Having empathy also means the educator understands

Parentship Success Team Agenda

Date:

Mission: (Develop your mission at the first few meetings and then state here for all future meetings.)

Vision: (Develop your vision at the first few meetings and then state here for all future meetings.)

Values (Collective Commitments): (Develop your values at the first few meetings and then state here for all future meetings.)

Goals: (Develop your goals early on in the process of creating your PST and then state here for all future meetings.)

Norms: (Develop your norms at the first few meetings and then state here for all future meetings.)

   1.

   2.

   3.

   4.

Old business:

New business on how the parentships can support student learning:

Follow-up action steps needed:

Next meeting:

Figure 2.1: PST sample agenda.

Visit go.SolutionTree.com/PLCbooks for a free reproducible version of this figure.

Team members (Diverse group representing all school departments):

Parent Co-Chair:	Principal Co-Chair:
Parent Member:	Parent Member:
School Member:	School Member:
School Member:	School Member:

Figure 2.2: PST sample team structure.

Visit go.SolutionTree.com/PLCbooks for a free reproducible version of this figure.

some of the challenges or limitations parents face. It also means educators truly believe parents can support student learning and that partnership can be grown through collaboration. The following insights about parents and caregivers will help educators do this.

- Parents will protect their young and often "bring out the claws" when they feel like their children are being attacked, mistreated, or misrepresented. A team of neuroscientists (Figner, 2021) found that love is what makes the difference when parents decide between protecting their young and self-preservation. This team noted the hormone oxytocin is continually released through interactions between parents and their children and when a parent feels their child is endangered. As an educator, understanding why this happens may provide you with more insight (and patience) when using the strategies laid out earlier in this book to defuse conflict situations. As a parent, also understand why you may become too protective and try to consciously make better choices with your behavior to handle situations as respectfully as possible.

- Parents want teachers to treat their children as if they were the teachers' very own. As a teacher, always ask yourself, "What would I do for my own child?"

- Understand that some parents have a bias against school—and that they might feel this way for good reason. You never know what parents experienced when they themselves were in school. Parents carry their individual histories with them, and their related feelings about school will likely remain as they raise their own children. They might have negative feelings about school, or they might not understand how things have changed or how school is supposed to be. Building bridges and partnerships requires an educator to acknowledge that these biases may exist.

- Understand that some parents come from communities that tend to not be as involved and are harder to engage than other parents. It is important to be more intentional with outreach to parents who have difficult circumstances to overcome.

Conclusion

Creating parentships to better engage and collaborate with parents will lead to numerous benefits: better, more positive relationships throughout the school; increased trust; improved communication; and improved student learning. These parentships start with the formation of the PST. It is important to understand the role that you as an educator will play in this process, as well as to have a better understanding of the role parents play. The next chapter explores the benefit of creating a shared mission and vision for your parentships.

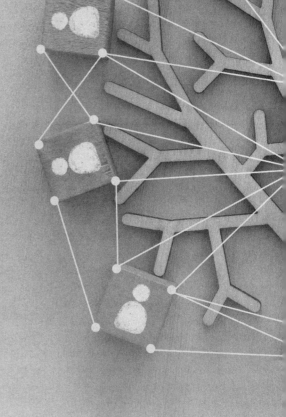

3

Creating Shared Mission and Vision Statements for Your Parentships

This chapter will describe how creating shared mission and vision statements specific to your parentships will provide the necessary purpose for why the parentships exist and the road map for where they are headed. Creating mission and vision statements is part of the work of the PST. The chapter will characterize why these statements are important to build your parentships, as well as ways to create and communicate the statements. Let's get started by exploring what mission and vision statements are.

There are only two ways to influence human behavior: you can manipulate it or you can inspire it.

—Simon Sinek

What Is a Shared Mission Statement?

Every organization, whether a business or a school, must define why it does what it does. Jim Collins and Bill Lazier (2020) describe an organization's mission as "a clear and compelling overall goal that serves as a focal point of effort" (p. 114). As Collins and Lazier (2020) note, a mission statement should be achievable as it translates values and purpose into an energizing, highly focused goal. It should be crisp, clear, bold, and exhilarating. Collins and Lazier (2020) push leaders to reject standard mission statements that look like carbon copies of one another and that comprise an assemblage of pretty phrases or a boring stream of words that evoke the response "True, but who cares?" (Collins & Lazier, 2020, p. 114).

In a PLC, a school's mission statement is the first leg of the table. According to Mike Mattos, Richard DuFour, Rebecca DuFour, Robert Eaker, and Thomas W. Many (2016):

> The mission pillar answers the question, Why do we exist? In a PLC, the mission—the fundamental purpose of the school—is to ensure high levels of learning for all, students and staff alike. This collective purpose sets the direction for the organization and serves as a compass to guide its actions. (p. 12)

To get to the heart of why schools exist, educators must reflect on the moral purpose of why they chose teaching as a career. Even though some school leaders assume they know why their teachers chose this profession, it's a discussion they still need to have with their staff as they work together to create a shared mission statement. Teaching requires a moral purpose, as teachers commit to serve and support students in any way they can. It should be crystal clear to all educators in a school that their work and passion must be compatible with the fundamental belief that all students must learn at high levels. That is the reason schools exist. Mission statements clarify priorities and sharpen focus. Following are a few examples of school mission statements.

- "Our mission is to ensure high levels of learning for all students."
- "Our purpose is to provide a safe and creative school environment by building positive relationships resulting in high academic and social achievement for ALL students."

Just like your school's mission statement, your parentship mission statement must define the fundamental purpose. The mission statement helps to build a foundation of *why* partnering with parents is so important and to establish that fact for the whole school community. Following are examples of parentship mission statements.

- "Our parentship mission is to collaborate with our parent community to ensure high levels of learning for all students."
- "Our parentship purpose is to provide a school environment driven by collaboration between school staff and parents resulting in high academic and social achievement for ALL students."

Later in this chapter, you will find a process for writing this mission statement.

Pause and Ponder

Why is partnering with parents important to you as a school leader or teacher?

What Is a Shared Vision Statement?

A shared vision focuses your organization, as well as the energy of the people in the organization. The Founding Associates and Consulting Partners of the Ken Blanchard Companies (2010) paint a picture of how research has consistently supported over time the idea that great leaders' essential characteristic is their ability to mobilize people behind an inspirational shared vision. A shared vision should also lead team members to determine what exactly the school or team can *stop* doing. In other words, it'll help everyone create a stop-doing list. When everyone in your organization reflects on what it is you are trying to become, it is easier to recognize what will help you achieve that goal and what will not.

In a PLC, a school's vision statement is the second leg of the table. A vision statement describes what the school wants to become in the future. The vision pillar asks, "What?"—that is, "What must we become in order to accomplish our fundamental purpose?" (DuFour et al., 2016, p. 39).

The whole idea is to facilitate collaborative conversations among staff to try to pin down something that is hard to define—the future. Educators Kenneth C. Williams and Tom Hierck (2015) describe the vision in a PLC as the *eye*, what staff use to envision and create a clear description for the school they seek to become.

In *The Five Disciplines of PLC Leaders*, Timothy D. Kanold (2011) offers this about a school's vision: "Vision moves the school organization beyond the question of *why* we exist to the question of *what* we should become" (p. 11). Kanold (2011) adds:

> Vision answers the question, are we really doing work that matters? Vision provides the focus and coherence necessary to avoid the natural drift toward mediocrity and stagnation. Vision describes how good we can become, and paints a picture of what it will look like when we get there. (p. 12)

Following are examples of school vision statements.

- "Our vision is to ensure every student is fully engaged and challenged through rigorous learning experiences that will prepare them for their future."

- "Palmer Elementary commits to creating future-ready students ready to thrive in the 21st century."

Involving parents in the visioning process is a powerful way to position yourselves as partners in the education process. Unfortunately, many educators and even some leaders view writing a vision statement—or a mission statement, for that matter—as a waste of time. This is usually due to the school's failure to identify the vision statement as the driving force for the right work in a PLC. If the connection isn't explicit, staff may think, "If we are not going to use this, then why create it?"

Writing a vision statement only to check it off the PLC to-do list is a seductive shortcut in the process of building your PLC. A shared vision statement must be so compelling it captures the hearts and minds of everyone in your school or district. As author Jon Gordon (2018) explains, "When *everyone* who influences the team gets on the bus together with a shared vision and greater purpose, the team becomes an unstoppable force of momentum and positive energy" (p. 40).

Just like your school's vision statement, your parentship vision statement must specify what your school hopes the parentships will become. It should not just include sweeping generalities; instead, it should be realistic, credible, and attractive to inspire the school community to live out the shared vision. The parentship vision statement must clearly illustrate what is next, and it must empower all members of the school community to do everything in their power to fulfill this vision. Following are examples of parentship vision statements.

- "Our parentship vision is to ensure all educators and parents are working together to ensure every student is fully engaged and challenged through rigorous learning experiences that will prepare them for their future."

- "The Palmer Elementary parentships commit to creating future-ready students ready to thrive in the 21st century by aligning our work together to best support students."

Pause and Ponder

What are your thoughts on engaging parents to help envision what your school or district should become in the future? What are the potential strengths of and challenges to this type of parental engagement?

Why Mission and Vision Are Important to Parentships

Brené Brown (2018a) captures the idea of clarity very well: "Clear is kind. Unclear is unkind" (p. 48). If you want parentships to become a driving force in your school community, you must ensure a high level of community awareness among staff. But you must then move beyond community awareness so that everyone more fully grasps the concept of parentships. That is, you don't want parentships to be something educators and parents are merely aware of; you want to foster a deep commitment to parentships, which requires a keen understanding of the why, how, and what of parentships. People cannot commit to what is unknown to them or what they are unsure about. Cultivating a deep understanding of parentships among staff and parents will ensure their comfort with the work and help them rally around it.

How to Create and Communicate the Mission and Vision

It is important to note that the process of writing mission and vision statements should not take forever. As PLC at Work experts Robert Eaker and Janel Keating (2012) note:

> While it's important to build a deep foundation for PLC practices, we have also learned the importance of not wallowing in the work—that is, not spending a tremendous amount of time on things that should be completed fairly quickly. (p. 28)

Mission and vision statements can be short or long. According to Mattos and colleagues (2016), "The length of the statement is not nearly as important as ensuring the statement is shared and it captures the staff's hopes and dreams for the future" (p. 22).

Mattos and colleagues (2016) indicate that most mission statements are approximately three to four sentences long, specifically identifying how the school will follow through on the fundamental purpose of all schools: student learning. Williams and Hierck (2015) promote the idea of crafting a powerful supplemental three- to five-word *mantra* "as another way to reconnect to your mission and serve as a triggered reminder—hearing the mantra will make your team immediately recall the mission" and work each day toward actions that support it (pp. 47–48). But you are not simply developing a catchy slogan; the message must have meaning.

After you've organized the PST, the team should meet to create the parentships' shared mission and vision statements. The following eight steps outline the mission- and vision-writing process.

Step 1: Create a Timeline

Begin by determining a timeline. First, establish the date by which you will complete the process—beginning with the end in mind. You shouldn't shortcut the process, but you also shouldn't take more than a few months to complete the mission and vision. The longer your school is without a parentship mission, the harder it is for all stakeholders to focus their energy on the fundamental purpose of student learning. Once the timeline is complete, send invitations to all members of the PST with the meeting dates, times, and locations. If some members of the team can't make it in person, invite them through Zoom or Microsoft Teams. You may also decide to offer a virtual meeting only to accommodate your busy parents and educators.

Step 2: Brainstorm

Prior to the first PST meeting, affix three pieces of chart paper to the walls around your meeting room. Also have plenty of pens, pencils, and sticky notes available for PST members. Once the meeting begins, lay out your expectations and goals, and ask team members to describe why creating a parentship mission and vision statement is so important to them. Divide the group into three smaller groups numbered 1 to 3, each with its own designated piece of chart paper. Once these groups have gathered together, give them five to seven minutes to start the brainstorming process by first answering the following three questions for mission statement creation. Follow this process to create your parentship mission statement and then do your parentship vision statement. Do not try to do both at one time.

1. Why do we exist?

2. What is the most important thing we need to do?

3. How can we most positively impact our students?

Later, when you create the vision statement, refer to these three reflective questions.

1. What do we want to become?

2. What is going to be important in the future for our students?

3. What skills and knowledge will our students need in the future?

At the end of the allotted time, have team members come back together as a team for ten minutes to share out each group's conversation. Have one member from each group share their group's ideas with the entire PST.

Step 3: Create the Survey

The survey should ask for feedback on the questions from step 2. PST members must volunteer for different roles in this process. Someone must set up the survey; another volunteer or volunteers will communicate the survey to parents and staff, along with reminders; and someone should provide technology support for those who need it. Paper copies can also be made to make it easier to collect feedback. Later on, PST members will analyze data and look for patterns in the feedback.

Step 4: Conduct the Survey

Establish a timeline for the survey window with a clear deadline. It is now time to push out the survey via electronic communication and disperse paper copies around the school to be available to staff and to parents at school events. The paper copies could also be sent home in student folders. The electronic survey should be sent out via email and Twitter, and be placed on the school website for easy access. After the original email is sent out, send out reminder emails every three to five days and then daily as the deadline for the survey approaches. The team should seek to get feedback from at least 50 percent of the parent community and 100 percent of the staff.

Step 5: Collect and Analyze Feedback

Once members have collected feedback, the PST comes together again to analyze the results, looking for patterns in the feedback and breaking down those patterns. The responses from parents and teachers will become the primary pieces to the new mission and vision statements. The team will also use the reflective questions in figures 3.1 and 3.2 (page 40), in addition to themes from the feedback, to create the new parentship mission and vision statements.

Reflect on the following questions to help create a mission statement that will steer your parentships.

1. How can we involve parents in the process to support student learning?

2. Do parents see our staff focusing daily on student learning?

3. If we were to run into a stranger and ask about our school, what would we like that person to say?

4. How are we involving parents and other community members in this process?

5. What would our school look like if parents were a vital part of our success?

6. What will accountability look like so we know we are meeting student needs on a daily basis?

7. If we were to create the school that we all want right now, what would it look like? What would it sound like? How would parents and staff be talking about the school?

8. Is the mission statement written well enough so that those who are part of our school understand what they must do to create the school we want?

9. In what ways will we communicate our shared mission statement? In what ways will we continue to reflect on our shared mission statement to ensure it has meaning?

Figure 3.1: Questions to guide the mission-writing process.

*Visit **go.SolutionTree.com/PLCbooks** for a free reproducible version of this figure.*

When working on the parentship vision statement, reflect on the following questions to help create a vision statement that will steer your parentships.

1. How would we like to see parents involved in the success of our school and our students?

2. How would we like for people to describe our school in three years? In five years?

3. How are we involving parents and other community members in this process?

4. What do we want our students to be equipped to do in the future so they are successful in life?

5. What would our school look like if parents were a vital part of our success?

6. What would our school look like if it was an extremely warm and caring place for students, staff, and parents?

7. What will accountability look like so we can create the school we all want?

8. If we'll have created the school that we all want five years from now, what will be different? What will be the same?

9. Is the shared vision statement written well enough so that those who are part of our school understand what they must do to create the school we want?

10. In what ways will we communicate our shared vision statement? In what ways will we continue to reflect on our shared vision statement to ensure it has meaning?

Figure 3.2: Questions to guide the vision-writing process.

*Visit **go.SolutionTree.com/PLCbooks** for a free reproducible version of this figure.*

Step 6: Draft New Statements

The team should not worry about length as they begin crafting the new statements. Members should work together to eventually condense the statements into forms that parents and staff will remember, speak, and act on.

Step 7: Finalize and Reflect

After taking a few weeks to reflect on the work they've undertaken, the team should reconvene to finalize the statements. Along with the final versions of the mission and vision statements, the team should identify ways staff and parents can both live the mission and use the vision statement to move forward.

Step 8: Communicate the Final Statements

Once your PST has finalized the mission and vision statements, disseminate them to the entire community in several ways, and post them in multiple locations—for example, in the school's front office and teachers' lounge, on a wall at the front of the building, on the school website, in staff email signatures, on PST agendas, and even on magnets that could be sent home to all families. Utilizing multiple forms of communication will help build knowledge and understanding of your parentships and hopefully lead to more buy-in and commitment among those in your school community.

Pause and Ponder

Do you believe these processes could be implemented in your PLC? What could you add or change to make them work for you and your school community?

Conclusion

Creating mission and vision statements will provide a strong compass for your school's parentships and assist in implementing the work more deeply into your school culture. Focused and purposeful mission and vision statements will lead to better collaboration and engagement with parents. Establishing exactly why your parentships exist and what you hope for them to become is vital to success and the potential to positively affect student achievement. Mission and vision statements are a great place to start, but you must follow them with accompanying actions. If your statements and actions align, parental engagement will soon follow.

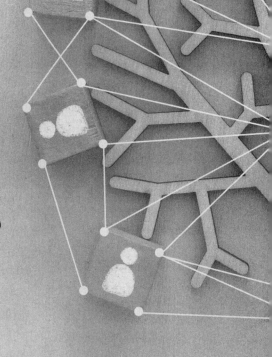

4

Creating Values and Goals for Your Parentships

This chapter describes the why and the how for creating values, or collective commitments, for your parentships. The specific attitudes and behaviors your values emphasize will make clear how educators and parents must act to honor and advance the shared mission and vision. This chapter also discusses how goals add accountability and allow you to monitor the success of your parentships in your PLC, as well as how you can communicate commitment statements and established goals for improvement. Let's start with how to clearly fulfill the values of your PLC.

> *What you do has far greater impact than what you say.*
>
> —Stephen Covey

Values (Collective Commitments)

Values are the third pillar. For a PLC to operate smoothly and carry out its mission and vision, members must establish—and hold one another accountable for adhering to—collective commitments in the form of norms that support its mission and vision. *Norms* are the specific behaviors and attitudes that members pledge to adopt as they work together in collaboration toward the right work in a PLC. In other words, these types of collective commitments answer the question "How must we behave to create the school that will achieve our purpose?" (DuFour et al., 2016, p. 41). They help individuals understand exactly how they can contribute to the success of the PLC. Members' fully understanding the purpose, direction, and core beliefs of the organization will lead to greater commitment, as well as actions that align with the success of all students in the school.

In a PLC, the principal is not the sole leader but rather a *leader of leaders*. Therefore, it is not just the principal who must ensure members keep their commitments. Just like players of great sports teams, members of a PLC understand that true teamwork involves *many* leaders who will hold one another accountable and insist that all members do their part to fulfill the mission and vision. If values are to impact the organization in a positive way, the people within the organization must, according to writer Adam Bryant (2014), "live by them, reinforce them every day, and not tolerate behavior that is at odds with them."

Just like your PLC has created collective commitments and collaborative team norms, your PST must create collective commitments that specify the behaviors that will guide the parentships. Parentship collective commitments must establish exactly how members of the PST will act toward one another as they lead the development and improvement of the parentship initiative in your building, but they will also serve to guide parents' and educators' interactions with each other within the broader parentships. Parentship collective commitments should be based on established common ground between parent and educator needs. Following are examples of collective commitments and norms.

- "I will commit to collaborating with my colleagues to ensure we are implementing a guaranteed and viable curriculum."

- "I will assume best intentions from my colleagues and help create a sense of belonging."

- "I will hold myself and others to high, rigorous expectations in the classroom."

- "Teachers will commit to:
    □ Use best practices daily in the classroom to stimulate student engagement
    □ Provide evidence of lesson and unit planning
    □ Engage in the PLC cycle of learning with my collaborative team
    □ Use common pacing guides in year-long instructional planning"

Pause and Ponder

What are two or three collective commitments you would like your school's parentships to establish?

Goals

The final foundational PLC pillar is goals. Goals help to provide benchmarks for success and to determine whether the PLC is indeed making strides in student achievement. Data analysis as it relates to the agreed-on goals will result in invaluable feedback for the continuous-improvement model. The right goals identify targets and timelines and will enable staff to answer the question "What results do we seek, and how will we know we are making progress?" (Mattos et al., 2016, p. 25).

Goals provide short-term focus to help staff make daily decisions and adjustments to their work to improve student learning. Goals align to the third big idea of a PLC—a results orientation—and provide each and every member direction on how to achieve better results. Goals are absolutely vital to the success of every collaborative team in a PLC.

Meaningful goal setting allows educators to set priorities and specific timelines for action that align to district and state goals as well. In *Every School, Every Team, Every Classroom*, Eaker and Keating (2012) outline several guidelines to follow to ensure success in this goal-setting endeavor:

- Goals should be tied directly to student achievement.

- Goals should be connected directly to the district's core purpose, vision, and values and commitments.

- Goals should be collaboratively developed.

- Goals should be clearly communicated and widely distributed.

- Goals should be utilized for decision making.

- Progress toward attaining the goals should be frequently monitored, coupled with specific feedback.

- Appropriate resources for attaining the goals should be provided.

- A consistent format for goals should be utilized across the district to ensure consistency and quality. (p. 30)

As leadership expert Zig Ziglar (2019) points out, "A goal properly set is halfway reached" (p. 56). And as authors Anne E. Conzemius and Jan O'Neill (2014) explain, goals should be SMART—that is, strategic and specific, measurable, attainable, results oriented, and time bound. Goals should focus on student learning, and schools should keep goals to a minimum, as the more goals you have, the less you can realistically focus on them.

Mirroring the way your school creates goals to identify targets and timelines for improvement, your parentship initiative will create goals on which people can provide feedback, track progress, and ultimately gauge the success of the parentships. Parentship goals will lay out exactly how your PST can monitor its work and provide data to help the group decide on the next steps for enhancing the parentship initiative in your building. Your team should write goals to assess the positive effect of the building's shared mission and vision statements and the collective commitments. In addition, goals should monitor student learning levels, as well as student attendance. They should also be able to assess parent engagement and involvement at school events.

To write meaningful goals to monitor incremental improvement for your parentship initiative, teams should follow the SMART-R goal-writing process. In addition to being written to be strategic and specific, measurable, attainable, results oriented, and time bound (Conzemius & O'Neill, 2014), goals should be written to *reinforce* the relationships between parents and educators in your parentships. For example:

- Eighty-five percent of parents can state or find the school's parentship collective commitments by January 1.

- Eighty percent of parents will indicate a score of four or five on the Parentships Perception Survey for the category "I consistently see school actions that align to the parentship mission statement" by May 1.

- Ninety percent of parents will support and follow their school's parentship norms on a consistent basis by May 1.

Pause and Ponder

How can you ensure SMART-R goals reinforce relationships between parents and educators?

Why Collective Commitments and Goals Are Important to Parentships

Collective commitments are essential for your parentship initiative. All stakeholders must understand the identified behaviors that will support the parentships, and when you explicitly lay out acceptable behavior in advance, it is easier for parents and educators to meet those expectations. Author and educational consultant Michael Roberts (2020) cites this as "a clear movement to the *we* culture of a PLC" (p. 44). The dynamic between parents and educators can be difficult at times, and providing this clarity up front will promote positive interactions between the two parties. Difficulties can commonly occur around what is best to do for students because of the different perspectives a parent and an educator often have and the roles they play. Difficulties could also occur with concern that parents are becoming too involved or possibly making decisions that typically teachers make.

In *Kid by Kid, Skill by Skill*, Eaker and Keating (2015) express the benefits the school community reaps from members' engagement in a collaborative process to develop collective commitments—and how this engagement can ultimately transform the building's very culture. Keating (as cited in Eaker & Keating, 2015) describes how, to help her colleagues commit to the power of PLCs, she commonly asks questions like "What would it look like [in our schools] if we really meant it when we said our fundamental purpose is to ensure all students learn? What would people see us doing?"

What would it look like if we really meant it when we said we embrace learning as our fundamental purpose, or we will build a collaborative culture, or we will use evidence of results to respond to student needs and improve our practice?

Goals for your parentship initiative are important as well. Goals will provide the clear expectations and the means for monitoring success that you will need in order to understand the current reality of the parentships. Monitoring goals will allow for feedback on the accuracy of timelines, as well as data about success in parental involvement and engagement. Parentships are meant to increase parental engagement, and the only way to truly see whether they are working as intended is to monitor their impact on your PLC. PLC experts Jeanne Spiller and Karen Power (2019) contend that school goals can create synergy. They go on to state that those who set the goals will find more opportunities to celebrate success because they are documenting more evidence-based actions.

How to Create and Communicate Collective Commitments and Goals

After the PST has created the shared mission and vision statements for the parentship initiative, it's time to write your collective commitments and goals. Before taking on this project, it is essential to establish some common ground between parents and educators that will provide representation for both parties and identify areas for which collective commitments can be written.

Common ground for collective commitments allows for a framework of values that supports both parents and educators in the goal of supporting student learning.

Failure Is a Positive

First, both parents and educators must understand that students learn from failure. In fact, failure can be one of the most productive forms of learning. Learning from failure is a skill students need to be successful not only in their schoolwork but also in life. As author J. K. Rowling (as cited in Satara,

2018) has said, "Failure is so important. We speak about success all the time. It is the ability to resist failure or use failure that often leads to greater success." Educational psychologist Michele Borba (2016) describes how failure is part of life, and if students don't have the opportunity to fail, they will never be able to rebound from making mistakes. This hinders their ability to build resilience.

Students Need Diverse Skills

Next, parents and educators must understand that students need diverse skills to thrive in the future. Students must be well equipped with a number of *soft skills*, such as the abilities to collaborate, think critically, adapt, harness creativity, and innovate, and they must demonstrate mastery of foundational but rigorous academic skills. Students must be prepared for lives that will be volatile, complex, uncertain, and at times scary.

Students Learn Behaviors From Adults

Finally, both parents and educators must understand that students need to learn positive behaviors from the adults they interact with the most: those at home and at school. Educators must ensure they are in a strong emotional state to enable them to act in a positive way. Being in a strong emotional state means that the educator knows the work is hard and stressful, but also feels that it is fulfilling and rewarding. No matter their age, a student is not able to have a higher emotional state than that of the adult in the classroom. Likewise, parents must be careful not to exude a negative emotional state. If an adult is emotional, the student will be in a similar or even lower emotional state. Students mimic adult behaviors. Amy Morin (2021) provides two reasons why this happens. First, Morin references the Social Learning Theory that clarifies people learn by watching others. In addition, Morin references the famous Bobo doll experiment in which children learned to imitate adult behavior by watching how the adults treated the doll. The children then treated the doll in the same manner. What actions of yours will they mimic?

Pause and Ponder

How can you and your school help to establish the parents' perspective for all staff in your building so that they truly appreciate the parent community?

How to Create Values (Collective Commitments)

The following eight steps outline the collective commitment creation process. The section ends with an easy-to-follow reproducible tool to aid you and your team in this process.

Step 1: Define the Process and Effective Commitments

The PST should know the process for developing values from beginning to end. This is also a good time to review the qualities of effective commitments. Roberts (2020) summarizes the qualities of effective commitments very succinctly.

- **They are manageable in number and easy to recall:** "If there are too many, the staff [and parents] will lose track of them and the organization's effort will be diluted" (p. 45). Commitments that can be mentally chunked and broken down are easier to recall. *Mentally chunked* refers to statements that may not follow proper sentence structure, but the shortness of the message makes it easier to remember and commit to memory.

- **They are measurable:** Measurability makes commitments more concrete so educators can more easily ascertain whether they are meeting them and on their way to accomplishing the mission and vision.

- **They have controllability:** Focusing on skills and behaviors that teachers or parents cannot control independently or only focusing on the parent or the educator will lead to frustration. As you will see in step 2, it is important to create commitments that both the parent and educator can control or that align to common ground.

Step 2: Review Areas of Common Ground

This is a good time to review the elements of common ground for educators and parents. Collective commitments should be behaviors that both parents and educators can exhibit. The three areas of common ground are as follows. (See page 47 in the previous section for details on these areas.)

1. Students need to learn from failure.

2. Students need diverse skills to thrive in the future.

3. Students need to learn positive behaviors from adults.

Step 3: Review the Mission and Vision

Restate your shared mission and vision so that they will be fresh in the minds of team members as they work through the process of creating collective commitments. Consider posting the shared mission and vision statements for all team members to easily reference. Clarify that the collective commitments the team creates and establishes will specifically describe how members of the parentships must behave to create the school you desire (shared vision) to achieve your purpose as a school (shared mission).

Step 4: Brainstorm Collaboratively

Next, the team breaks down the specific behaviors needed to fulfill the shared mission and vision. The team should work collaboratively to list these behaviors on a whiteboard or poster paper for all to see. Examples of behaviors your PST may write include the following.

- "We will collaborate together as parents and educators to communicate honestly and appropriately at all times."
- "I, as an educator, will commit to honoring and listening to the voices of parents on our PST."
- "I, as a parent, will commit to honoring and listening to the voices of educators on our PST."

Step 5: Categorize and Write

The team should categorize the listed behaviors into the corresponding common-ground areas. Then the PST should break into three subgroups, with each subgroup assigned to write collective commitments for one of the common-ground areas. Subgroups should take fifteen to twenty minutes to write one or two collective commitments for their common-ground areas based on the listed behaviors.

- "I will commit to being an active and available member of this PST by attending all meetings and fulfilling any responsibilities asked of me."
- "I will commit to making decisions that are student-centered."
- "I will commit to supporting a decision once it is made."

Step 6: Get Feedback

Reconvene as one group and combine all the collective commitments into one document divided by common-ground area. The co-chairs of the PST, along with the building principal, should then provide the copy of collective commitments to the school community of parents and educators for input.

The best way to do this is through a Google Form survey to elicit specific feedback on the following six items.

1. Are the commitments written as behaviors needed to fulfill the shared mission and vision?

2. Are the commitments written to align to the common-ground areas they are listed under?

3. Are the commitments written so both parents and educators can conform to the behavior?

4. Are the commitments few enough or chunked enough so others can easily understand them and conform to them?

5. Can both parents and educators control the commitments?

6. Are the commitments measurable?

Step 7: Revise the Values

Give educators and parents two to three weeks before collecting feedback. The PST should then review all feedback and make appropriate corrections to the parentship collective commitments to finalize them. If a commitment received a lot of questions or negative feedback, the team should revise or delete it. Based on feedback, the PST may need to add a commitment. The PST should use any feedback that is sensible and in some way provides direction in their future actions.

Step 8: Communicate the Values

Communicate your collective commitments frequently and in multiple locations, such as in the front office and teachers' lounge, on a wall at the front of the school building, on the school website, in staff email signatures, and on PST agendas. Additionally, these values should appear on signs as parents enter spaces like the auditorium, cafeteria, and other large common areas in your school. You can also list parentship goals in your school-improvement plan or, in your conference room or another similar area, on charts where you can graph advancements. Utilizing multiple forms of communication will help build knowledge and understanding of your parentships and hopefully lead to more buy-in and commitment among those in your school community.

Figure 4.1 (page 52) is a template to help your parentship team create collective commitments.

Common Ground

1. Students need to learn from failure.

2. Students need diverse skills to thrive in the future.

3. Students need to learn positive behaviors from adults.

Mission:

Vision:

Behaviors needed to fulfill your shared mission and vision:

Collective Commitments (CC; First Draft)

1. Students need to learn from failure.

   CC 1—

   CC 2—

2. Students need diverse skills to thrive in the future.

   CC 1—

   CC 2—

3. Students need to learn positive behaviors from adults.

   CC 1—

   CC 2—

Final Parentship Collective Commitments

1. Students need to learn from failure.

   CC 1—

   CC 2—

2. Students need diverse skills to thrive in the future.

   CC 1—

   CC 2—

3. Students need to learn positive behaviors from adults.

   CC 1—

   CC 2—

Figure 4.1: Parentship collective commitment writing process.

Visit go.SolutionTree.com/PLCbooks for a free reproducible version of this figure.

How to Write SMART-R Goals

Parentship goals will provide specific timelines and expectations so you can measure whether you're making incremental improvements toward the success of your parentships. You'll be able to see what is or is not working for each parentship strategy you implement.

The following three steps outline the goal-writing process. The section ends with a reproducible tool to aid you and your PST with this effort.

Step 1: Outline Areas for Success

Begin by outlining exactly which areas you want to monitor to assess the parentships' effectiveness. Though you and your PST might identify other key indicators as well, it will be critical for you to track the effectiveness of the:

- Mission statement
- Vision statement
- Values (collective commitments)
- Student-learning strategies
- Student-attendance strategies
- Parent-attendance strategies (for school events such as parent-teacher conferences, back-to-school nights, information nights, assemblies, fine arts performances, and so on)

Step 2: Understand the Current Reality

To write goals that will capture the appropriate timelines for action and completion, as well as ways to monitor your parentships' success, you must first understand your current reality. You and your team must have honest conversations about those same key performance indicators and evaluate them accordingly. *Learning by Doing* (DuFour et al., 2016) provides great continua to accurately reflect on your current reality so you and your team have an accurate understanding of where you currently stand as a school in numerous areas.

Step 3: Establish Goals

Utilizing the same process for writing SMART goals in a PLC, you and your team should write goals with an added emphasis on the parent perspective. As mentioned previously, SMART goals are specific and strategically aligned with school and district goals, measurable, attainable, results oriented (that is, requiring evidence of higher levels of student learning in order to be achieved), and time bound (Conzemius & O'Neill, 2014). DuFour and colleagues (2016) explain that schools and districts should pursue SMART goals to help them monitor and celebrate incremental improvement toward achieving the organization's vision and mission.

Remember—in order to connect your parentships to meaningful goals to monitor incremental improvement, you should follow the SMART-R goal-writing process (see figure 4.2). That is, in addition to possessing the afore-mentioned qualities, your goals should reinforce the *relationships* between parents and educators in your parentships.

Pause and Ponder

What are your goals for your building's parentships?

Identify Key Indicators for Parentship Success

1.

2.

3.

4.

5.

6.

Current Reality

Of first key indicator:

Of second key indicator:

Of third key indicator:

Of fourth key indicator:

Of fifth key indicator:

Of sixth key indicator:

SMART-R Template

S: Is the goal strategic and specific?

M: Is the goal measurable?

A: Is the goal attainable?

R: Is the goal written as results oriented?

T: Is the goal time bound?

R: Does the goal reinforce the relationship between parents and educators?

Figure 4.2: Parentship goal-writing process.

*Visit **go.SolutionTree.com/PLCbooks** for a free reproducible version of this figure.*

The "SMART-R Goal Template to Track Parentship Goals" (see the reproducible tool on page 56) will help the PST establish a plan for action steps, accountability, timelines, and evidence of success for each goal the team sets.

Conclusion

The establishment of values, or collective commitments, and goals will provide strong guidance for your school parentships, help to drive the parentship work more deeply into your school culture and climate, and lead to more positive behaviors from and interactions between educators and parents.

SMART-R Goal Template to Track Parentship Goals

Action Steps (What specifically needs to happen to achieve the SMART-R goal?)	Accountability (Who is responsible for carrying out these actions?)	Timeline Targets (When do these actions need to be followed up on?)	Evidence of Success (How will we know these actions have led to improvement?)
SMART-R goal to measure effectiveness of the mission statement:			
SMART-R goal to measure effectiveness of the vision statement:			
SMART-R goal to measure effectiveness of the values (collective commitments):			
SMART-R goal to measure effectiveness of student-learning strategies:			
SMART-R goal to measure effectiveness of student-attendance strategies:			
SMART-R goal to measure effectiveness of parent-attendance strategies:			

Part 2

STRATEGIES FOR PARENTSHIPS IN A PLC

The chapters in part 2 of this book provide strategies for building your parentships. Each chapter presents first school-driven strategies (implemented at the school level) and then team-driven strategies (implemented in the classroom). Dividing approaches in this way will help you and your school delineate exactly who will take the lead on developing and executing strategies. Each chapter ends with a Think, Plan, and Act section for teams to use when trying a specific strategy from the chapter.

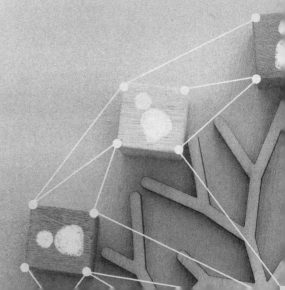

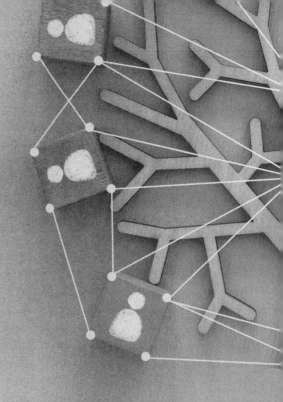

Strategies Related to Curriculum

This chapter explores strategies that help your parentship initiative support student learning, specifically related to curriculum. It describes school-driven strategies and team-driven strategies. Each strategy provides thorough details on how you and your colleagues can replicate the strategy and implement it in your school or classroom.

The only impossible journey is the one you never begin.

—Tony Robbins

School-Driven Strategies

The strategies in this section will help you and your team foster essential student learning outcomes.

- Parentship universe portal
- Career navigators

Parentship Universe Portal

Many school districts already use a parent portal of some sort. Commonly used parent portals such as PowerSchool, Infinite Campus, Gradelink, and Skyward exist as warehouses of student data. This student management software also serves to provide parents with similar information, giving them direct access to student attendance, the daily gradebook, owed fees, the class schedule, and report cards. According to a PowerSchool (2021) study:

> There are usually three things parents are looking to stay informed
> about in the school life of their students. They want to know about

assignments and when they are due, they want to see grades, and they want to see their child's work.

In addition, the PowerSchool (2021) survey reveals that 76 percent of teachers and administrators feel technology is a critical tool for communication and 71 percent feel a personalized mobile learning app helps tremendously in communication. People can download apps to a phone or tablet—an extremely easy, convenient way to access information. Portals such as these are a powerful way to provide parents with real live data about students, and all districts should utilize them.

Though the decision to use a parent portal may be up to the district, if you do not currently use such an information system, please be an advocate for its acquisition. If your district is unable or unwilling to invest in a districtwide student-information portal, you can create one on your building's website. There are several free website creators and templates you can use as a starting point. To do this, add a page or access point to your school website that offers the following information.

- Student attendance

- Student grades

- Student progress reports (report cards)

- Student daily schedule

- Curriculum materials

  - Essential grade-level or content-area learning outcomes

  - Grade-level or content-area pacing guides

  - Grade-level or content-area supplemental materials (from the state or district)

- Schoolwide and team-based SMART goals and tracking updates

- Parent resource links

  - ACT (https://act.org)

  - Attendance Works (www.attendanceworks.org)

  - College Board (www.collegeboard.org)

  - Edutopia (www.edutopia.org)

  - Every Person Influences Children (www.epicforchildren.org)

  - Families in Schools (www.familiesinschools.org)

  - Khan Academy (www.khanacademy.org)

  - National Association of Elementary School Principals (www.naesp.org)

- ☐ National Association of Secondary School Principals (www.nassp.org)

- ☐ National Center for Learning Disabilities (www.ncld.org)

- ☐ National PTA (www.pta.org)

- Parent collaborative (see chapter 7, page 77, for more information)

  - ☐ Agendas and presentations

- Commonly asked questions and answers

- PST

  - ☐ Team mission, vision, values (collective commitments), and goals

Career Navigators

Career navigators are parent volunteers in the school community trained by school personnel to assist students and families in making postsecondary decisions involving college, career technical institutes, entrepreneurship opportunities, and so on. The main advantage to career navigators is that they are currently, or very recently, working in the particular career they will help others navigate. This strategy tends to be more appropriate at the secondary level, but this type of parental engagement can also benefit families with students in middle or elementary school, providing them with early access to educational and career-related information and a deep personal connection that can boost students' future readiness. This early entry into important career-oriented discussions would be a welcome addition to various projects and learning experiences suitable for younger students. As the American Institutes for Research (2021) note, career and technical education is a critical strategy for preparing students and adults for future education and workforce opportunities. Making use of parent career navigators is a much-needed way to help students negotiate these sometimes difficult choices. The following items detail the specifics of the parent career navigator strategy.

- **Role:** Career navigators support building activities related to the execution of real-world learning opportunities for students, as well as serve as mentors or advisers for students and families as they approach decision making about college and other postsecondary opportunities.

- **Who:** Any parent or community member can serve as a career navigator as long as they have been background checked and trained on the essential functions of the role by appropriate school personnel such as those in the counseling office. Schools should recruit a diverse group of individuals to establish a wide range of professions and careers.

- **Collaboration:** Career navigators work with your school's counselors or other staff who guide the career-pathway and postsecondary programming on your campus. These identified school staff will provide training to the navigators and relay volunteers' contact information to parents who would like to request their counsel. Parents then specifically request support based on their students' interest and skills. Parents will also have access to the appropriate information to make these contacts. Oftentimes, parents may feel more comfortable talking with other parents or community members than with school personnel, who may have less experience in specific career areas.

- **Communication:** Career navigators will choose the extent of their involvement in this process; they can offer their cell phone numbers or email addresses so that parents can contact them directly, or they can have the school counselor contact them whenever someone is interested in working with or talking to them.

- **Formation:** Use the template in figure 5.1 to advertise the need for career navigators in your building. Announce it on your school's website, include information in weekly school and teacher newsletters, post about it on Twitter and Facebook, and so on. Try to create as diverse a team as possible to represent numerous professions, career choices, and opportunities.

The use of career navigators is appropriate at all school levels. In high school, this resource could be used for students who are close to graduating. In middle school, this would be a great opportunity to begin to get students interested in certain careers. In elementary school, career navigators can be involved in project-based learning experiences to help students understand how the volunteer's career connects to reading, English, mathematics, and science skills.

Pause and Ponder

What ideas do you have about implementing these school-driven strategies in your building?

Attention Parents and Guardians,

We have an awesome opportunity for many of you to get involved in our school this year: become a career navigator, helping other students and families with very important decisions about life after high school.

Career navigators are parents (and other community members) who volunteer their time and expertise to serve as sounding boards for other parents as they make important decisions about their children's futures.

Career navigators serve as mentors or advisers for students and families as they approach decision making about college and other postsecondary options.

If this interests you, please follow the link to the Google Form to provide your name, best contact information, and current occupation or career-exploration support area. Once you submit your information, you will be listed as a contact for other families to reach out to for advice and other feedback.

[provide Google Form link here]

Thank you for supporting our students and families!

Figure 5.1: Parent career navigator request letter.

Visit **go.SolutionTree.com/PLCbooks** *for a free reproducible version of this figure.*

Team-Driven Strategies

The following strategies will help your PST and other collaborative teams establish ways to support your students' learning in relation to essential content-area or grade-level learning outcomes. The team-driven strategies for this chapter are:

- Interactive homework
- College and career student panels

Interactive Homework

Interactive homework is homework that requires students to engage their parents, guardians, or other caregivers. These assignments are more than just parents assisting with students' understanding of concepts. Instead, interactive homework qualifies how parents, guardians, or caregivers will connect with students for the homework assignment. The idea is to bring parents and students closer together through collaborative exercises. Writer Michael Alison Chandler (2013) describes a study by Emory University that found that the greater children's knowledge of their family histories, the more positive their outcomes, including healthier levels of self-esteem, strong beliefs in their capacity to control their futures, lower levels of anxiety, fewer behavioral problems, more resilience in the event of hardship, better academic performance, and improved relationships with their parents.

Compared to traditional homework, interactive homework:

- Is assigned less frequently

- Provides specific questions and activities that require a family member to not only assist but participate

- Builds relationships between students and their parents, guardians, or other caregivers

- Requires the teacher to follow up on the successes and challenges of the assignment and to provide a space for parent feedback

- Offers prompts and ideas for parents to engage with students during the activities

- Is more project based and offers multiple days or weeks for completion

- Connects to parent experiences that can help students get to know their parents better

- Ties into lifelong learning opportunities that are important for students to understand and that offer a bridge to their futures

Examples of interactive homework include:

- Family members completing an interactive writing activity that highlights the parent's life

- Family members watching a YouTube video together and discussing what they learned

- Family members discussing the best ways each of them learns and what is required for all of them to have successful learning opportunities

- Student retelling a story and parent making a connection to a real-life experience they have had

- Parent providing a writing prompt to the student, giving him or her one hour for completion

- Family members going on a scavenger hunt around the house, trying to find as many angles and shapes as they can and checking items off an established list

Figure 5.2 will help you and your team prepare interactive homework for parents and students, ensuring parental engagement that will support and increase student learning.

Interactive Homework to Be Assigned	Timeline for Interactive Homework	Goals for Parent-Student Interaction	Follow-Up From Teacher

Figure 5.2: Interactive-homework design.

*Visit **go.SolutionTree.com/PLCbooks** for a free reproducible version of this figure.*

College and Career Student Panels

In an effort to support students and families in making postsecondary decisions, you can organize student panels to provide more vital information to families. As we all know, many students and families struggle with these types of decisions. While the school counseling team can handle financial aid and admissions questions, with this strategy, families can seek feedback from former students who have recently graduated and had similar experiences. Here are items to consider when planning a student panel.

- **What:** The panel should consist of a variety of students who have made different choices, such as those who currently attend four-year universities, two-year junior colleges, and career and technical schools, as well as entrepreneurs, those who have entered into apprenticeships, those enlisted in the military, and so on.

- **How:** School staff most familiar with the overall student population, such as counselors and administrators, should select students who fit the criteria. The best way to do this is to recruit students as they are graduating, in preparation for future panel opportunities. But as you begin to create these panels, you will need to reach out to graduates, ideally those who live close by. To get in touch with those students, use your connections— for example, talk to younger siblings currently enrolled in your school, parents and community members, and others. Social media is also a great tool for recruiting students for panels. Note, too, that panels can be a combination of virtual and in-person gatherings.

- **Why:** This strategy allows for authentic feedback about how to best make decisions about postsecondary life, as panel members discuss the challenges and barriers they've faced, as well as positive experiences. The audience will most likely be senior students, but anyone in high school should be offered the opportunity to attend the panels. Of course parents and guardians are invited as well.

- **When:** Offer college and career panels throughout the entire school year, but concentrate them more heavily in the fall of each school year. A possible schedule would include a panel in September, November, January, and March. Schedule these panels well in advance, and plan to hold them in the evening. Recording these events will be helpful to those who are unable to attend. Place the recordings on the parent portal for all to access. I also recommend advertising that former students will be attending so families know some background to ensure their interests match panel members.

- **Topics:** Panel topics can include scholarships, entrance-exam preparation, application processes, final school selection process, general college preparation, real-world successes and failures, positives and negatives of different choices, and so forth.

Figure 5.3 will help you and your team organize students to serve on the panel you are developing.

Pause and Ponder

What are potential challenges to implementing these team-driven strategies? How can you work to overcome those challenges?

Panel members:

Name and career: College:

Name and career: College:

Name and career: College:

Name and career: College:

Member of the military: Junior college:

Entrepreneur: Technical school:

Entrepreneur: Technical school:

Panel date, location, and time: (Advertise well in advance, noting virtual, in person, or both.)

Date:

Location:

Virtual or in-person:

Topics: (For example, scholarships, college selection process, entrance exams, college or technical school preparation, application processes, career choices, career preparation, successes and failures, positives and negatives, entrepreneurial aspirations)

Figure 5.3: Planning tool for college and career student panels.

*Visit **go.SolutionTree.com/PLCbooks** for a free reproducible version of this figure.*

Think, Plan, and Act

Use the "Planning, Implementing, and Monitoring Tool for Curriculum Strategies" document (see the reproducible on page 68) to bring clarity to the process of planning for and implementing new parentship initiatives. Remember to keep your focus narrow, putting your energy into one or two parentship initiatives at a time.

To use the tool, start by picking a strategy and identifying who is responsible for leading the strategy. Next, determine the resources needed, list specific action steps for successfully implementing the strategy, and think about something you can stop doing to ensure you have the time to properly focus on implementation. Finally, follow up on the success of the strategy by scanning for signs of positive impact.

Planning, Implementing, and Monitoring Tool for Curriculum Strategies

Strategy	Is It School or Team Based?	What Resources Are Needed?	What Action Steps Will We Take to Implement the Strategy?	What Could We Stop Doing to Make Time?	What Are the Signs of Positive Impact Following Implementation?

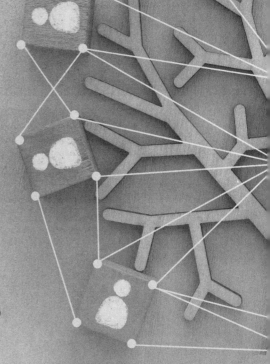

6

Strategies Related to Individual Student Progress

This chapter explores strategies that will help your parentship initiative better support individual student progress. The material that follows will connect back to your mission by providing strategies that will make that mission—improved student learning—a reality. No matter where students are academically, they all can advance in their learning.

Alone, we can do so little. Together we can do so much.

—Helen Keller

School-Driven Strategies

The school-driven strategies in this chapter are as follows.

- Parent-teacher conference framework

- Student-attendance family support

- Translators

Parent-Teacher Conference Framework

Parent-teacher conferences are a great way for parents and educators to connect to discuss how each student is doing in school. Though high attendance at these events is important, many schools find that attendance is not at the level they'd like. Jeremy Monk (2018) of the Council of Ministers of Education, Canada, notes that the parental engagement that comes with parent-teacher conferences "allows for greater understanding of expectations, challenges and ways to improve the school experience." He adds that conferences are crucial for students' academic and behavioral development because the resulting conversations shed light on any unique challenges the students may be facing in the classroom.

Conferences are often short, ranging from ten to twenty minutes on average. That does not leave a lot of time for discussion, so I offer the following framework to help you use that time as efficiently as possible. This framework strategy will help you not only streamline the parent-teacher conference to ensure you communicate the most important content but also increase overall parent attendance at the conferences. I also encourage you to involve students in parent-teacher conferences—no matter the grade level. The students should be the focus; therefore, they should be present.

Elementary Framework

1. Lead introductions.

2. Share one celebration and one overall student-growth goal (in collaboration with the student).

3. Have a conversation focused on the four critical questions of a PLC.

   a. What does the student need to know? (Focus on essential learning outcomes for main content areas.)

   b. How is the student doing with these essential learning outcomes?

   c. What is the student doing at school to help them better understand these essential learning outcomes? What can the parent do at home to provide support?

   d. What is the student doing because they already understand the essential learning outcomes?

4. Establish the following commitments.

   a. The student makes a commitment for their own progress.

   b. The parent makes a commitment for student progress.

   c. The teacher makes a commitment for student progress.

The framework for secondary conferences differs since students and families meet with numerous teachers.

Secondary Framework

1. Lead introductions.

2. Have a conversation focused on the four critical questions of a PLC.

   a. What does the student need to know? (Focus on essential learning outcomes for main content areas.)

b. How is the student doing with these essential learning outcomes?

c. What is the student doing at school to help them understand these essential learning outcomes? What can the parent do at home to provide support?

d. What is the student doing because they already understand the essential learning outcomes?

3. Establish the following commitments.

a. The student makes a commitment for their own progress.

b. The parent makes a commitment for student progress.

c. The teacher makes a commitment for student progress.

I encourage all schools and school leaders to continue to allow for the possibility of virtual conferences. As we learned during the COVID-19 pandemic, virtual meetings can and do work. What we have found consistently across the United States, for example, is that parent-teacher conference attendance has increased dramatically because of the ease of connecting online and attending regardless of work schedules, childcare needs, transportation, and so on. Video conferencing helped to increase participation in these often under-attended events and will continue to give busy parents more opportunities to engage (Bentley, 2021). Figure 6.1 is a tool to use during elementary and secondary parent-teacher conferences in your building.

Introductions (one minute)	
Celebrations and Student-Growth Goals (three minutes)	
What does the student need to know? (four minutes)	Essential-Learning-Outcome Focus Areas
How is the student doing with learning these essential learning outcomes? (four minutes)	Evidence of Learning
What is the school doing to support the student's learning, and what can parents do at home to help? (four minutes)	Strategies Used to Support Learning Not Yet Acquired
What is the student doing if they already know the essential learning outcomes? (two minutes)	Extension Opportunities
One Commitment Each From Student, Parent, and Teacher (two minutes)	Commitments: 1. Student— 2. Parent— 3. Teacher—

Figure 6.1: Parentship parent-teacher conference planning tool.

*Visit **go.SolutionTree.com/PLCbooks** for a free reproducible version of this figure.*

Student-Attendance Family Support

Poor attendance can have dramatic negative consequences. Research by the nonprofit GreatSchools (2011) suggests "that the consequences of low attendance are serious for all children and for the community, not just the students who miss school." Students who have chronic absenteeism problems fall behind in academics, get into trouble with the law, and cause other problems in their communities (GreatSchools, 2011).

Figure 6.2 shows a three-phase attendance-improvement process. This strategy for student-attendance family support includes a system of interventions focused primarily on students' families to help provide a remedy for attendance concerns that arise with chronically absent students. Typically, phase 1 students need universal first-step strategies to help them be more successful with their attendance. Phase 2 students need earlier, more purposeful interventions for their attendance problems. Phase 3 students need intensive interventions from numerous school staff, such as building administrators, counselors, social workers, nurses, and classroom teachers.

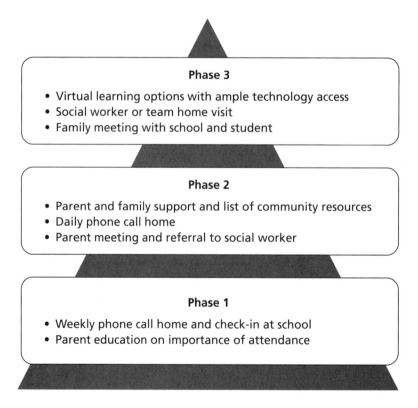

Phase 3
- Virtual learning options with ample technology access
- Social worker or team home visit
- Family meeting with school and student

Phase 2
- Parent and family support and list of community resources
- Daily phone call home
- Parent meeting and referral to social worker

Phase 1
- Weekly phone call home and check-in at school
- Parent education on importance of attendance

Figure 6.2: Three phases of attendance-improvement strategies.

To address attendance concerns, you need to drill deeply to correctly diagnose the cause, which might include any of the following.

- Lack of transportation (no vehicle or money for gas)

- Academic issues (problems with teachers, poor academic performance, fear of failure, disciplinary action, suspension)

- Social-emotional issues (gender intimidation, bullying, difficult peer relationships, anxiety, depression)

- Family issues (financial problems, conflict with parents, lack of parents or guardians at home, too many responsibilities, violence in the home or community, child-rearing, homelessness, abuse, poor health, family member's poor health)

Use figure 6.3 to track the success of phase 1, 2, and 3 interventions that you implement with students with chronic absenteeism problems.

Student	Factors Impacting Student Absenteeism	Phase 1, 2, or 3?	Which Intervention?	Success of Intervention and Next Steps	Communication Log and Notes

Figure 6.3: Planning tool for student-attendance family support.

*Visit **go.SolutionTree.com/PLCbooks** for a free reproducible version of this figure.*

Translators

Almost one in four children in the United States (more than twelve million) speaks a language other than English at home (Scamman, 2018; Statistica, 2022). Most schools and districts have designated on-site staff who can provide language translation for parent meetings, phone calls, and the like. Oftentimes, these staff are very busy and cannot be available when needed most. Schools also use contracted services to help with translation. This is great as well. What I suggest is that school leaders also pay a stipend to staff who can speak multiple languages so they, too, can be called on to provide translation when needed. The translator could be an office clerk, a counselor, a teacher, or a custodian. The more resources you have, the better you will be able to communicate with families who don't speak English. With the assistance of interpreters and translators in education settings, educators can ensure that students with families who are learning English receive the language support they need to progress in school (Scamman, 2018). Note that such staff can also help translate written materials. It may also be possible to include parents or community volunteers to help with translation services.

Pause and Ponder

How do these school-driven strategies compare to what you currently do in your school? How could you make changes to fully implement one of these strategies?

Team-Driven Strategies

The team-driven strategies to support individual student progress are:

- Virtual teacher office hours
- Email from students

Virtual Teacher Office Hours

Your communication with parents is essential to student success. One way to enhance communication is to make yourself more available to parents who have questions. Virtual office hours are a weekly opportunity for parents to reach out to teachers for help and assistance in their own efforts to support student learning at home. A great advantage to parents is that they know exactly when the teacher will be available and can try to schedule their day to make themselves available during the teacher office hours.

I recommend that each member of the collaborative teacher team take on the responsibility of office hours for one week every month, rather than every teacher putting in this extra time every week. Since collaborative teams in a PLC should be on the same page with regard to essential learning outcomes, assessments, and the guaranteed and viable curriculum, every teacher on the team should be ready and able to assist. However, questions specific to a particular classroom or student need must ultimately be directed to the student's classroom teacher.

In singleton or smaller teams, members may be able to provide virtual office hours only once or twice a month. Schools may also find a way for teachers to meet these commitments by trading time from other commitments—that is, they might be allowed late arrival one day or early release on a Friday afternoon, tasked with fewer duties, relieved of recess coverage, and so on.

Email From Students

In the 21st century, this strategy should be easy to implement, as it involves students sending weekly Friday emails to their parents or guardians. This additional communication updates parents and guardians about the week, student progress, celebrations, and struggles at school, as well as reminds parents of important upcoming dates. The main purpose of the email is for students to share how they have performed or progressed in their learning over the course of the week.

Caregivers should respond to students' emails, copying the teachers who monitor the communication. This can be done in elementary schools (as Friday seatwork) and secondary schools (during advisory time or in one specified class each Friday).

Pause and Ponder

Knowing time is always of the essence, what are some things you could stop doing to provide more time for parent communication?

Think, Plan, and Act

Use the "Planning, Implementing, and Monitoring Tool for Student-Progress Strategies" (page 76) to bring clarity to the process of planning for and implementing new parentship initiatives. Remember to keep your focus narrow, putting your energy into one or two parentship initiatives at a time.

To use the tool, start by picking a strategy and identifying who is responsible for leading the strategy. Next, determine the resources needed, list specific action steps for successfully implementing the strategy, and think about something you can stop doing to ensure you have the time to properly focus on implementation. Finally, follow up on the success of the strategy by scanning for signs of positive impact.

Planning, Implementing, and Monitoring Tool for Student-Progress Strategies

Strategy	Is It School or Team Based?	What Resources Are Needed?	What Action Steps Will We Take to Implement the Strategy?	What Could We Stop Doing to Make Time?	What Are the Signs of Positive Impact Following Implementation?

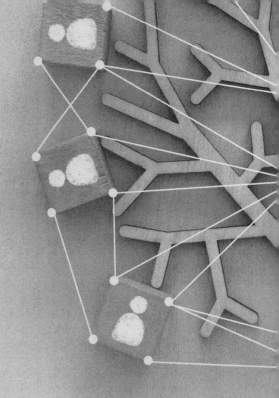

7

Strategies Related to Parental Engagement

This chapter explores strategies that will help your parentships better support parental engagement. As we have discussed in this book, sometimes parents don't know how to help. The school and team strategies in this chapter will assist educators with addressing that concern. Each strategy provides thorough details on how you and your colleagues can replicate the strategy and implement it in your school or classroom.

Teamwork is not a preference, it is a requirement.

—John Wooden

School-Driven Strategies

You will learn more about the following school-driven strategies in this chapter.

- Parent collaborative
- Front-office creed
- Schoolwide norms
- Livestream of school events
- Childcare at school events

Parent Collaborative

A parent collaborative is an established schedule of meetings, either in person or virtual, that provide vital information and training to your parent community. The parent collaborative also offers an avenue for parents to ask questions and inquire about information they need regarding calendar dates, grading, scheduling, career-pathway opportunities, and curricula. This strategy works at the early childhood and elementary, middle, and high school levels. This strategy aligns directly to the work of your PST; the team determines training topics based on areas of need identified through data analysis. Here are the specifics on the parent collaborative.

- **What:** The parent collaborative comprises weekly information sessions and trainings for parents.

- **Purpose:** These sessions and trainings help schools connect more deeply with their parent community, as well as provide a venue for parents to ask questions about matters ranging from grading to behavioral expectations.

- **Format:** Meetings can take place in person or electronically, via Zoom, Microsoft Teams, or another desired platform. In-person sessions should include refreshments for attendees and make childcare available to the parents who choose to come. Making childcare available is a great way to boost attendance.

- **Frequency:** Weekly sessions should be thirty to forty-five minutes in length and scheduled at various times throughout the month. For example, you might hold some sessions at noon, others at seven thirty in the morning, and others at five o'clock or later in the evening. A varied schedule will accommodate parents' schedules and needs.

- **Potential topics:** The possibilities for topics of discussion are numerous.

  - District-level student learning objectives and goals that align to the school's mission

  - Specific ideas and strategies the school is using to create the school they want to become (these trainings would align to the school's vision statement)

  - Remote learning

  - Racial equity and diversity

  - Students' social-emotional needs

  - How to maintain a supportive learning environment at home

  - Ways to connect with the school through the parentship universe portal and other means

  - Student-attendance support

       ☐ Social media and the traps and pitfalls of technology

       ☐ Drug use, signs of suicidal ideation, and other at-risk behaviors

Record and upload sessions to the parentship universe portal so parents can access the trainings at their convenience. Connecting all these resources for parents is an incredibly effective way to ensure the information you provide reaches as many parents as possible.

Front-Office Creed

It is imperative that the front office be a warm, caring, and highly functioning area of your school. First impressions mean so much to not only your staff and students but also your parents. One way that parents judge the effectiveness and impact of your school is by their experiences in the front office or on the phone with front-office staff. In K12 Insight's (n.d.) *2019 State of K–12 Customer Experience Report*, researchers find that building trust is the most important foundation for a successful community relationship. In addition, the report states that an ongoing and systemic approach to building a customer-service culture is what generates trust and, in turn, public confidence.

Because of the critical need for a warm, inviting atmosphere in the front office, staff must meet certain standards. Front-office staff primarily include administrative assistants, though sometimes other staff work from the front office—and behavioral expectations apply across the board. There is no doubt that operating in this area can be difficult, but the front office sets the tone for the building, contributing significantly to the culture and climate. Do not underestimate the need for positive, effective customer service in the front office. The building administration team, or those in charge of districtwide professional development, should carry out the training for front-office staff. Don't forget: treating your front-office staff with care allows them to better care for others.

This strategy involves front-office staff working together to create their own front-office creed, which will guide them in their daily work with the school and parent community. Figure 7.1 (page 80) is an example of a front-office creed. Try to schedule two or three meetings with front-office staff, before school starts if possible, to collaboratively work together to create your creed. The first step is to make sure everyone knows what the purpose of the creed is and how to create it. The next step is to brainstorm ideas. After you brainstorm ideas, put words to paper and create a rough draft of your office creed. After you do that, take a week or two to reflect and think about your creed. Then meet one final time to finalize the creed. Finally, create copies of the creed and a product for your wall to hang for all to see.

Statement of Excellence

Our school believes in the importance of our parents, students, and staff. Therefore, we want to ensure that, as front-office staff, we provide you with a world-class experience, because we know how important you are to this school. We believe that customer service is the most important thing we can offer as we take care of any needs or concerns you may have.

Commitment to Customer Service

We are happy to help you in any way we can. We will always prioritize our opportunity to work with you to address your questions, comments, and concerns. Although you may be having a bad day, our intention is to make it better.

Student Focus

As you are aware, our school exists to provide an excellent learning experience and environment for our students. We support staff so that they have more time to devote to their students in the classroom. We support parents so that you can not only better understand the processes and procedures specific to our school but further support your child at home. And, of course, we support our students because that's why we are all here!

Our Communication Will Be

- Honest
- Judgment-free
- Patient
- Thorough
- Positive

While Visiting the Front Office, You Can Expect To

- Be greeted with a smile
- Be offered water
- Receive solutions for your concerns
- Receive answers to your questions
- Experience a positive, warm environment

Figure 7.1: Example of a front-office creed.

*Visit **go.SolutionTree.com/PLCbooks** for a free reproducible version of this figure.*

Of course, to do this effectively, you must secure training for staff. Here are some possible training resources.

- SUPER heroes workshop (www.k12insight.com/trusted /pd-customer-service-training)

- Book studies of texts such as *Be Our Guest: Perfecting the Art of Customer Service* by Theodore Kinni, *The Starbucks Experience: 5 Principles for Turning Ordinary Into Extraordinary* by Joseph A. Michelli, and *How to Win Friends and Influence People* by Dale Carnegie

- Pryor Learning Solutions webinars (http://pryor .com/training-webinars)

Schoolwide Norms

Just as those in collaborative teacher teams should establish behavioral norms for interactions within and outside the group, schools should determine norms for parent meetings and schoolwide events. It is always best to be explicit about your expectations of others.

You'll need to lay out norms for:

- Meetings between teachers and parents or guardians

- Meetings between the principal and parents or guardians

- Interactions between front-office staff and parents or guardians

- Phone conversations between teachers and parents or guardians

- Phone conversations between the principal and parents or guardians

- Schoolwide community events, such as back-to-school night, parent orientation, kindergarten roundup, parent-teacher conferences, informational evenings, and so on

- All electronic meetings or events

When developing these common norms, please consider the following.

- If you have a PST, its members should collaboratively develop norms. If you don't have a PST, your school's PTA or PTO should outline them. It is important to involve parents in the establishment of schoolwide norms.

- Ensure that norms are always present in each setting by hanging posters, placing placards on tables, posting them on the school's website, reviewing them before events, and so on.

- Let others know when they are breaking norms by immediately reminding them of the established behaviors expected of everyone within the school setting.

Following are examples of schoolwide norms for events.

- "I will commit to treating others with respect and control my emotions at all times."

- "I will commit to always doing what is in the best interests of the student."

- "I will commit to saying only positive things about others around my student."

- "I will commit to calmly addressing any concerns I may have and understand how others may perceive me."

Livestream of School Events

To allow parents the chance to attend more events, begin (or continue) streaming school events virtually for the public and community. If your school already has the staffing and equipment to do this (for example, a broadcasting club or program), take advantage of it. If you don't have these resources and you want to start a broadcasting program, search for grants and apply school budgets and bond monies, if available. You will also need to reach out to a local media outlet or broadcasting company and gauge their interest in starting an internship program for added support. You may be able to offer your students value-added credentials to help in their college and career journeys.

If you believe students cannot be responsible for livestreaming, you are wrong. I have personally witnessed programs like this for my own child and in the school district in which I currently work. In partnership with a local media company, my district started a program only a few months before the writing of this book, and it is already a robust, exhilarating learning experience for students. Not only that, but it makes available to parents events they otherwise wouldn't be able to attend.

If you don't currently livestream events and don't have the financial resources to start a broadcasting program, it still may be easier than you think. There are many inexpensive ways to livestream events, such as with Periscope, Facebook Live, Livestream, Broadcast Me, StreamNow, Instagram Live Stories, Alively, and Twitch. All these applications are easy to use. Stream as many events as you can. Your community will thank you!

Childcare at School Events

Parents may be able to attend more school events if childcare is provided for young children. For example, parent-teacher conferences are situations in which distractions are not welcome. To address this barrier, your school can offer childcare for families. The benefits of this are twofold, as you (1) support families so they can make it to your school event and ultimately (2) nurture the parentships.

One relatively easy way to provide childcare is by using local high school students. High school students often need volunteer hours for school, church, National Honor Society, clubs, scholarships, and grants, to name a few. Foster these types of connections through the high school counselor or principal. In addition to seeking out high school students, you might also contact local churches, for example, for adult volunteers who are ready and willing to support schools in the community.

Be sure to communicate the childcare service in newsletters, as well as fliers for the school event. Have parents sign releases and provide contact information when they drop off children, and be aware of approximately how long the younger children will need care.

Finally, establish a location in your school that is not being used for the school event. It may be your gym, cafeteria, or art room. Identify one or two staff you can ask to supervise, and if payment is possible, that is a bonus. The cost will be small compared to the enormous support you will be providing to families.

> ## Pause and Ponder
>
> Which of these strategies has the biggest potential for positive change in your school? What would be your next steps for implementing the strategy?

Team-Driven Strategies

The team-driven strategies to support parental engagement are:

- Parentship promise
- Phone calls
- Volunteer invitations

Parentship Promise

Utilize the parentship-promise strategy to establish behavioral norms for school activities that involve the collaborative work of parents and educators. Either your PST or another group of parents and staff who serve to improve the parentships should develop the norms.

When creating norms for parent-educator events, consider scenarios and situations in which effectively developed and communicated norms will help. (See the Schoolwide Norms section on page 81 for scenarios and situations.)

Figure 7.2 (page 84) is a template to assist you in fully executing this strategy. Insert your school's norms to complete each "We promise to" statement, and have all parents and guardians and school staff acknowledge their understanding of the behavioral expectations for school events.

As a team, you need to do all you can to ensure you have received acknowledged parentship promises from all parents and guardians. Keep track of submissions, and follow up with individuals who have not signed the form. You can ask for paper copies to be returned or use an online acknowledgment form. Reference the parentship promise throughout the school year as often as you can.

As a school and parent community, we must establish high expectations for ourselves as we work collaboratively to make our school the best it can be! To help do this, a group of parents and educators at our school have identified the following behavioral norms to ensure we always maintain professionalism in our work together.

1. We promise to _____.

2. We promise to _____.

3. We promise to _____.

4. We promise to _____.

5. We promise to _____.

We ask that you acknowledge below that as a valued member of our team, you will commit to keeping these promises for our school community.

_____   _____
Parent Signature   Educator Signature

Figure 7.2: Parentship promise.

*Visit **go.SolutionTree.com/PLCbooks** for a free reproducible version of this figure.*

Phone Calls

This may seem like a strategy with which you're already familiar, but odds are, for most educators, they're making phone calls to parents less and less often due to the increasing demands of their job. One of the main concerns I see with new teachers as I work with them in my human resources position is establishing relationships with parents and being comfortable making phone calls to them. Phone calls can be a very effective way to communicate with parents and create more trust in your parentship initiative. According to Harvard education researchers Matthew Kraft and Shaun Dougherty (2013), frequent teacher-family communication immediately increases student engagement. Phone calls add a personal touch because the parent can hear your voice and understand better how much you care for their child. Emails, texts, and newsletters are still effective means of communicating with parents, but phone calls are very personal—especially when they serve to share good news and positive updates. Compared to email and social media correspondence, phone calls that relay positive news:

- Reassure parents that you see the good in the student

- Create a culture of celebration

- Build trust and relationships

- Ensure parents' receipt of the message

According to Kraft and Dougherty (2013), frequent phone calls and direct messages to parents increase the odds of students completing their homework by 40 percent, decrease instances in which teachers have to redirect students by 25 percent, and increase class participation rates by 15 percent. Communication through social media is generally less effective because it is not made directly to the parent. I recommend that elementary teachers plan to reach out to each parent or guardian with a personal phone call by October 1, secondary teachers by the end of December.

Within the workday, teachers can easily spend five to ten minutes speaking with two students' parents or guardians. That's ten students each week and your entire class each month. The biggest positive is that once you've established a solid relationship with a parent, if you must eventually call with negative news, the parent will already have a foundation of trust with you. That parent will know that you have the best intentions for the student. Figure 7.3 offers a script you can use when making phone calls to parents and guardians.

1. Introduce yourself and ask how the parent is doing.

   Good afternoon. This is _____, your child _____'s teacher. I can't tell you how awesome it is to have _____ in my classroom this year. How are you doing today?

2. Start with a celebration. (If this is the reason for the call, please elaborate on how much you enjoy the student in class.)

   I wanted to let you know that just the other day, _____ was able to _____. As you know, _____ has been struggling with _____ and is really working hard.

3. If applicable for the call, describe facts and actions, not your opinions.

   Although _____ has been really working hard, _____ had a problem today: _____.

4. If applicable, ask questions for support.

   I know this may come as a surprise to you. I knew that you would want to know what happened at school today. What can I help you with? Do you see behaviors like this at home? What have you done that helps with _____?

5. If applicable, provide solutions and resources.

   As I thought about this situation, I realized that, to me, it is more important that _____ learns from this and that we don't just have consequences. With that in mind, I am going to have _____.

6. Check to see whether the parent fully understands.

   I know I just said a lot. Does all this make sense to you? Do you have any questions or details that we need to revisit?

7. Ask for their partnership in working together for the betterment of the student.

   To really help _____ understand what happened today, I would appreciate your partnering with me and talking with _____ this afternoon when _____ gets home from school. It is important that _____ understands that we are on the same page and that we both want what is best for _____, developing the needed skills as _____ grows up. Have a great day!

Figure 7.3: Parent phone-call script.

*Visit **go.SolutionTree.com/PLCbooks** for a free reproducible version of this figure.*

Volunteer Invitations

All schools ask for parent volunteers, but they don't always convey just how much they need and appreciate those volunteers. Being intentional about how you reach out to your parent community will help you successfully find volunteers to assist in classrooms, on the PST, at school events, and so on. The PST can work alone or with the PTA or PTO to ensure an aligned effort toward volunteer recruitment. Figure 7.4 provides a sample volunteer invitation you can disseminate to your parent and school community.

Our school is committed to providing a world-class educational experience for your child. Did you know that adult volunteering in schools has actually declined over the past decade? We want our school to be different, and we need your help!

You are a valuable resource—in fact essential to the success of our school. You have something to offer our students and our school, whether it's your career experience, ability to lead other adults, patience in working one-on-one with students in the classroom, or specific skill or trade. We need your help, but we also know you are busy. Thankfully, volunteer commitments geared toward helping our students can look very different from one person to the next, as we need volunteers who can take on larger projects, as well as those who have a bit of time before or after school to complete smaller tasks.

Sue Shellenbarger (2018) of the *Wall Street Journal* has researched the impact of parent volunteering on students and finds that volunteering in your child's classroom or school has many positive impacts, such as higher student achievement, a strong sense of safety and security, and stronger relationships between parents and staff. Are you ready to make a difference?

If interested, please indicate below how you would like to help and the time you would be available to help. Remember—no time or role is too small to help our students succeed!

Name:

Contact information (phone and email address):

Child's name:

Talent to offer:

Time to offer:

Figure 7.4: Volunteer invitation.

*Visit **go.SolutionTree.com/PLCbooks** for a free reproducible version of this figure.*

Pause and Ponder

What are the most important aspects of these team-driven strategies? Do you believe following templates and scripts like these will help you in your parent-school communication?

Think, Plan, and Act

Use the "Planning, Implementing, and Monitoring Tool for Parent-Engagement Strategies" (page 88) to bring clarity to the process of planning for and implementing new parentship initiatives. Remember to keep your focus narrow, putting your energy into one or two parentship initiatives at a time.

To use the tool, start by picking a strategy and identifying who is responsible for leading the strategy. Next, determine the resources needed, list specific action steps for successfully implementing the strategy, and think about something you can stop doing to ensure you have the time to properly focus on implementation. Finally, follow up on the success of the strategy by scanning for signs of positive impact.

Planning, Implementing, and Monitoring Tool
for Parent-Engagement Strategies

Strategy	Is It School or Team Based?	What Resources Are Needed?	What Action Steps Will We Take to Implement the Strategy?	What Could We Stop Doing to Make Time?	What Are the Signs of Positive Impact Following Implementation?

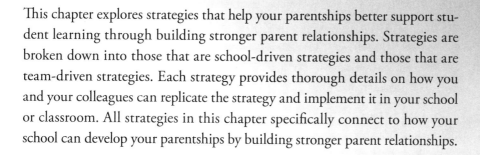

8

Strategies for Building Stronger Parent Relationships

This chapter explores strategies that help your parentships better support student learning through building stronger parent relationships. Strategies are broken down into those that are school-driven strategies and those that are team-driven strategies. Each strategy provides thorough details on how you and your colleagues can replicate the strategy and implement it in your school or classroom. All strategies in this chapter specifically connect to how your school can develop your parentships by building stronger parent relationships.

I want to make a difference with people who want to make a difference doing something that makes a difference.

—John C. Maxwell

School-Driven Strategies

The school-driven strategies in this chapter are:

- Parent ambassadors
- Bus tours and neighborhood visits
- Home visits

Parent Ambassadors

A parent ambassador is a parent or guardian in your school community who helps to spread the positive vibe about your school and to connect and communicate with other parents in an effort to create the best-possible school culture. Parent ambassadors specifically spread a positive vibe about your school by spreading the mission and vision statements and how they are being lived out in the school, and by exhibiting behaviors consistent with the school's values. Parent ambassadors are especially effective for acclimating parents who are new to the school community. The specific expectations of parent ambassadors are as follows.

- Meet with families who are new to the school to answer any questions they may have from the parent's perspective. Set up these meetings before or after scheduled school tours that school staff conduct, for example. This would also include new kindergarten parents in elementary school, parents of students entering middle school, and parents of students entering high school.

- Host a table at back-to-school events to ensure parents have access to community resources, such as local charities, churches, counseling and mental health facilities, area banks and real-estate agencies, a directory of apartment buildings, employment offices, health care locations, available transportation, and so on. These are of special interest to parents new to a geographic area.

- Be available for parents and guardians in the school community who wish to call with specific questions. Sometimes questions are better suited for other parents, as opposed to school staff and personnel, such as questions about specific school personnel, what the best way to go about contacting school staff is, and information about the general parent community.

Recruiting parent ambassadors can be part of your overall parent-volunteer campaign; however, parent ambassadors should possess certain characteristics. They should be able to communicate and influence others and have credibility and connections among the parent community, as well as the desire to be a strong positive voice for the school and what it stands for. See figure 8.1 to help build a team of parent ambassadors.

Bus Tours and Neighborhood Visits

Organizing a bus tour of your school boundaries has many advantages and can be done for various purposes. Here are potential ways to make the most of such a bus tour.

- Take a bus tour with your school staff to see the entire attendance area for your school. Include as many streets as possible. Taking a bus tour with your school staff will allow your staff to better understand where their students are coming from and gain proper empathy for the families in your boundary area. Taking a tour will also help to unite your staff with your community and

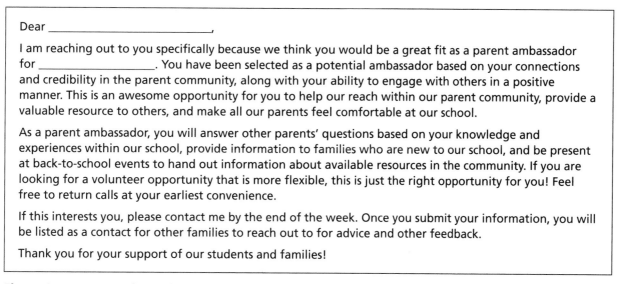

Figure 8.1: Parent ambassador recruitment template.

*Visit **go.SolutionTree.com/PLCbooks** for a free reproducible version of this figure.*

show your support for your community. The best time to do this would be immediately after school or on a Saturday morning if possible. When I was a principal, we did a tour like this at the beginning of the school year on a professional development day.

- Take a bus tour that stops at all the apartment buildings in your attendance area so teachers can read to students. (This strategy requires communication ahead of time so that families know when and where to congregate to listen.) You can also arrange for longer stops so that staff may provide homework assistance to students at various locations around the attendance area.

- Once a week in the summertime, plan a picnic where available staff will meet at a specified location to read to students and where students can enjoy light snacks and a few other activities. This would take approximately an hour and a half, and it does not need to be expensive. Look to community businesses to donate snacks. The real value is the time spent among staff, students, and families.

Home Visits

Visiting families' homes and working to build stronger relationships with families is a great way to close the connection gap with parents. This also helps to build stronger parentships. Making home visits to students' families can be incredibly beneficial. This strategy is especially useful for connecting with parents who are otherwise uninvolved or who aren't sure how to request resources or information from the school.

Home visits are about introducing yourself to families and getting to know them better. Talking with families outside the school setting can be more relaxing and conducive to building a connection. Home visits help families immediately understand that you care for them and are looking out for their best interests. By dedicating your time and energy to home visits, you will effectively communicate the importance of maintaining strong parentships.

Home visits are also a great opportunity to deliver resources and supplies to families in need. Parents may feel embarrassed or unwelcome when asking for that kind of assistance. They also may not have the means to travel to the school or other sites to get the help they need. Delivery via school personnel is a direct way to bridge the gap and ensure students have items such as backpacks, school supplies, food, and so on.

Finally, with this strategy, teachers have the opportunity to see students and their families in a whole new light. This added context will be invaluable as you work toward the success of all students.

Typically, the school administration team, counselor, social worker, and any other staff who want to volunteer compose the home-visit team. You could also invite parent ambassadors and other parent volunteers. Conducting home visits is an excellent way to commit to the school's mission, so hopefully you mobilize plenty of volunteers. When participating in home visits, clearly mark your vehicle with a magnet of your school logo so that parents recognize who is approaching their home.

Utilize all the communication tools you can to help home visits be more effective and efficient. Have the school secretary print addresses on Google Maps so residences are easily identified and close to one another. Advertise your visits so parents and the community expect you. Once word spreads, more families will even come to see you or visit with you as you are doing home visits. Of course, you would also hope these home visits make families know they matter so they will seek out more opportunities to be present at school events and in their own child's learning. Some families may be uncomfortable with you entering their homes, which is fine. Being inside the home is not the point. Simply talking with family members outside their front door is sufficient. Also, families generally don't like surprise visits, which is why communicating ahead of time is critical.

It's easier to conduct home visits in the summertime as the new school year approaches. You can still organize them during the school year, just not as frequently. Be creative with coverage to ensure some staff are always available to pay visits. Counselors, social workers, and school-engagement specialists are great potential candidates for home visits, especially those scheduled during the school year.

Note that you should do everything in your power to ensure safety on your visits. Do this by announcing your presence in advance; taking a security officer with you; clearly marking yourself as a school employee by wearing your badge; quickly identifying yourself verbally; and, again, having a school magnet on your car to identify you as a member of the school you represent. Use figure 8.2 to help you get organized for your home visits. Fill out this form for each visit.

Need	Details
Student	Augustus C.
Address	15 Main Street
	(Provide Google Map printout with directions from school.)
Purpose	Student needs back-to-school materials (bag, folders, pencils, paper, scissors, glue, and so on).
Checklist	☐ Family has been given advanced notice.
	☐ Magnet is attached to car for recognition.
	☐ Staff identification is present.
	☐ Script is accessible (if applicable).
	☐ Materials are ready for home delivery.
Staff in attendance	☐ School administration
	☐ School counselor
	☐ School social worker
	☐ Teacher
	☐ Family outreach coordinator
	☐ Parent ambassador

Figure 8.2: Home-visit template.

*Visit **go.SolutionTree.com/PLCbooks** for a free reproducible version of this figure.*

Pause and Ponder

Do you believe you have parents in your school community who would be valuable ambassadors to others? Can you think of better ways to enlist their help?

Team-Driven Strategies

The team-driven strategies for reaching out to parents are:

- Heroes in the home
- SOAP program

Heroes in the Home

The heroes-in-the-home strategy has two purposes. The first is to celebrate diversity among students and families, which can lead to further conversations about racial equity. The second is to draw the connection between students and their parents so the former see the latter as positive role models, which will strengthen relationships within the family. Note that grandparents, aunts and uncles, and adult mentors close to the family can be heroes in the home as well.

To implement this strategy, teachers will need to designate a wall in the classroom as a parent wall. Students then bring in pictures of their heroes to display on the wall. This strategy will work at any level—elementary, middle, or high school.

In their lesson planning, teachers should include time for students to share throughout the week or month. Do not feel the need to have all students share at one time. It is best to spread out the heroes-in-the-home discussions so that they can lead to conversations about racial equity throughout the whole year. To enhance learning for all the students, parents can also visit the classroom during these times. Use figure 8.3 to help facilitate this activity in your own classroom.

Step	Notes
Introduce parent, guardian, or adult mentor. (two to three minutes)	The student introduces their hero in the home by stating the person's name, relationship to the student, and as much information about the individual as the student can. If present, the hero in the home can also add to this description.
Focus on the why. (three to five minutes)	The student describes why they chose this particular person, explaining why the person is their hero and what the hero's relationship means to the student.
Initiate racial-equity discussion. (ten minutes)	The teacher leads the class in a discussion by asking the hero in the home the following questions. • What do you celebrate in your culture that may be different from other cultures? • How has your race impacted your life? • In what ways have you fought for racial equity in your life and in your role? • What is one thing you want all our students to know about racial justice? • What is one thing you would recommend we do to achieve more racial justice in our lives?

Figure 8.3: Heroes-in-the-home framework.

*Visit **go.SolutionTree.com/PLCbooks** for a free reproducible version of this figure.*

SOAP Program

The SOAP, or support one awesome parent, program provides an opportunity for staff to partner up with specific parents who are in need of support, encouragement, or just better connections to the school.

Interested staff sign up to participate in this program, and school administration leads a process to identify parents in need. The PST could also reach out to parents who would like extra support. Support might involve staff occasionally sending emails or making phone calls to parents—checking in and asking whether they need anything, inviting them to meet in person to talk, offering encouragement, and ensuring parents are aware of all the resources the school or community provides. Staff should do whatever they feel comfortable doing to support parents.

Pause and Ponder

What information do you need in order to best implement these team-driven strategies and identify parents and guardians who would benefit from outreach efforts?

Think, Plan, and Act

Use the "Planning, Implementing, and Monitoring Tool for Parent-Outreach Strategies" (page 96) to bring clarity to the process of planning for and implementing new parentship initiatives. Remember to keep your focus narrow, putting your energy into one or two parentship initiatives at a time.

To use the tool, start by picking a strategy and identifying who is responsible for leading the strategy. Next, determine the resources needed, list specific action steps for successfully implementing the strategy, and think about something you can stop doing to ensure you have the time to properly focus on implementation. Finally, follow up on the success of the strategy by scanning for signs of positive impact.

Planning, Implementing, and Monitoring
Tool for Parent-Outreach Strategies

Strategy	Is It School or Team Based?	What Resources Are Needed?	What Action Steps Will We Take to Implement the Strategy?	What Could We Stop Doing to Make Time?	What Are the Signs of Positive Impact Following Implementation?

9

Strategies for Monitoring and Sustaining Your Parentships

In this chapter, we'll explore the importance of monitoring your parentships' success, as well as strategies for sustaining it. Are the parentship strategies you've implemented working effectively and bringing about positive results? Are your parentship initiatives in fact tenable; will the school be able to maintain them over the course of years? The surveys and continua of this chapter will help you ensure the success and longevity of your parentships.

Greatness is not a function of circumstance. Greatness, it turns out, is largely a matter of conscious choice.

—Jim Collins

Monitoring Parentships

What gets monitored gets done. This adage holds true for so many things, including the development of your parentships. Simply announcing a new initiative or even beginning a new initiative does not guarantee its long-term success. According to professors Jeffrey Pfeffer and Robert I. Sutton (2000), decisions alone do nothing to promote and guarantee success unless you put in place mechanisms to monitor the strategy's implementation.

DuFour and colleagues (2016) clarify one of the most important and frequent questions effective leaders of the PLC process ask: "How do we know?" This question also applies to monitoring the effectiveness of parentships. When we constantly ask ourselves, "How do we know?" we remind ourselves to diligently review products and other evidence of teamwork and schoolwork to monitor the effectiveness of the parentship implementation.

When schools start PLC work, the "goal is not to become a PLC; the goal is to significantly enhance the learning of all students throughout the district—in every school and in every classroom" (Mattos et al., 2016, p. 140). The same holds true for your work in establishing your parentship initiative. When schools undertake this work, the goal is not to become parentships; the goal is to significantly enhance the partnership between parents and educators to ensure all students have the best resources and supports to improve their learning.

> ## Pause and Ponder
>
> Why is monitoring the work of your parentships important to you? How will monitoring this work help you?

Monitoring the Success of Your Parentships

There are many effective ways to monitor how your parentship implementation is going in your school community. This section discusses the following three ways.

1. Reviewing products

2. Reviewing feedback

3. Checking goals and timelines

Reviewing Products

As your school works to develop the parentships and implement initiatives, pore over the products that come from that work. This evidence serves as one of the best ways for you to look deeply into the actions of your teams and see exactly what is working and what is not working. Products from the parentship work of teams and schools must demonstrate what they have done to improve parentships. For example, evidence from a high-functioning and positive front office helps to create an environment where parents immediately feel welcome in the school. Look at evidence of the valuable information parent ambassadors are providing to other parents.

Reviewing Feedback

Each spring, survey your parents and school community to obtain feedback on how the parentship initiative is progressing. How does the community feel about the mission, vision, values (collective commitments), and goals? Are they having an impact? Are actions for improvement aligned to the building mission, vision, values, and goals?

It would be disrespectful and insincere to ask parents and staff to share their thoughts and then do nothing with their feedback. Therefore, once you have received survey results, share them with your school community. The PST should extensively look over the results, condense them into main takeaways, and then create corresponding action plans to address the areas that warrant improvement. Also be sure to celebrate by sharing positive feedback on the parentships' work. In this chapter, there are also two continua that deal with the mission and vision that should be filled out based on feedback from the perception survey. Reviewing the feedback is the best way to seek out the current status of the parentships and then plot out the next steps for improvement.

Pause and Ponder

What are other ways you can monitor the effectiveness of your parentships?

Figure 9.1 presents an easy-to-use parentship-perception survey you can distribute to get informative feedback from your parent community and monitor the success of your parentships. You can design this survey as a Google Form or use any other technology tool you deem appropriate. (See the reproducible tool on page 109.)

Please respond to the following prompts to provide our parentship success team with valuable information on the progress of our goal of building stronger parentships in our school community.	Please indicate your response by circling a number from 1 to 5, where 1 means *strongly disagree* and 5 means *strongly agree*.				
Mission Statement					
I can state my child's school's parentship mission statement.	1	2	3	4	5
I consistently see school actions that align to the parentship mission statement.	1	2	3	4	5
I believe my child's school's fundamental purpose is high levels of student learning.	1	2	3	4	5
My child's teachers call me consistently throughout the school year.	1	2	3	4	5
If I need something, I feel confident I can contact the school and staff will provide a resource I need.	1	2	3	4	5
Vision Statement					
I can state my child's school's parentship vision statement.	1	2	3	4	5
I consistently see school actions that align to the parentship vision statement.	1	2	3	4	5
I believe my child's school is working hard to create a school to better meet my child's needs.	1	2	3	4	5
My child's school tries to involve me in important collaboration, such as volunteer opportunities, to help more students succeed.	1	2	3	4	5
My child's school often asks me for my feedback.	1	2	3	4	5

Figure 9.1: Parentship-perception survey.

continued →

Values (Collective Commitments)					
I can state or find my child's school's parentship collective commitments.	1	2	3	4	5
I consistently see school actions that align to the parentship collective commitments.	1	2	3	4	5
I believe my child's school is working hard to commit to the promises they make about behaviors and actions we should see from them.	1	2	3	4	5
I believe my child is better able to handle failure because of actions the school and I have partnered on to help my child grow and learn.	1	2	3	4	5
I believe my child is more prepared for the future because of actions the school and I have partnered on to help my child grow and learn.	1	2	3	4	5
I believe my child has learned positive behaviors because of the modeling the school and I have provided to help my child grow and learn.	1	2	3	4	5
I am invited to be a part of school events.	1	2	3	4	5
I feel welcome when I enter my child's school.	1	2	3	4	5

Use the parentship-perception-survey overview tool (figure 9.2, and reproducible on page 110) to help you collect and summarize the feedback you receive from the parentship-perception survey.

Number of Parent Responses (Total)	Number of Staff Responses (Total)	Celebrations	Areas of Improvement

Figure 9.2: Parentship-perception-survey overview tool.

Checking Goals and Timelines

In addition to reviewing feedback from the parentship-perception survey, the PST must also monitor the goals and timelines it has established to guide the parentships' work. According to Robert J. Marzano and Timothy Waters (2009), to be effective, schools and districts must continually monitor progress toward clearly defined goals. Teams and schools can use the SMART-R goal and timeline tracking template shown in figure 9.3 for this purpose. (See the reproducible tool on page 111.) The template also provides an opportunity for the PST to reflect on the strengths and weaknesses of the goal-reaching process and to determine what the next action steps should be.

Action Steps (What specifically needs to happen to achieve the SMART-R goal?)	Accountability (Who was responsible for implementing these actions?)	Timeline Targets (When did these actions need to be followed up on? Were they met?)	Evidence of Success (Was the goal met?)	Strengths and Weaknesses (What are the strengths and weaknesses of the goal-reaching process?)	Next Steps for Implementation (What are the next steps we will take?)
SMART-R goal to measure effectiveness of the mission statement:					
SMART-R goal to measure effectiveness of the vision statement:					
SMART-R goal to measure effectiveness of the values (collective commitments):					
SMART-R goal to measure effectiveness of student-learning strategies:					
SMART-R goal to measure effectiveness of student-attendance strategies:					
SMART-R goal to measure effectiveness of parent-attendance strategies:					

Figure 9.3: SMART-R goal and timeline tracking template.

Use the parentship mission statement continuum shown in figure 9.4 to monitor your current parentship shared mission statement and the meaning it carries in your school community. The PST should fill out this continuum each spring after receiving feedback on the parentship-perception survey.

Starting	Strengthening	Intentional	Impactful	Powerful
School staff established our parentship mission statement to describe a school that would be great to be part of and help students learn. The statement is displayed on the school website and on signs in the school.	School staff established our parentship mission statement to describe a school whose members would work collaboratively to take ownership of student learning. Staff recite the statement, and it is shared in multiple locations.	Our parentship mission statement describes how staff can commit to the fundamental purpose of the school: student learning. It is visible and discussed in meetings. Stakeholders came to a strong consensus in crafting the statement; staff understand it must mean something.	Our parentship mission statement describes how staff will commit to the fundamental purpose of the school: learning for all students, staff, and parents. It is visible in the school and used as a mode of celebration.	Our parentship mission statement describes what the staff have passionately committed to, the fundamental purpose of the school: learning for all students, staff, and parents. It is visible and discussed in multiple settings. Everyone understands the mission and works to fulfill it.
Staff did not involve parents in the process in any way.	Staff did involve parents in the process.	Staff involved parents in the process by eliciting their feedback on the statement.	Staff involved parents in the process by eliciting their feedback on the statement. Parents were present during the mission statement's writing.	Parents are a part of the PST and were integral to the writing process. Several parents provided feedback. Staff listened to parents, whose impact on the mission statement was significant.
Some staff know the mission statement, and staff actions are misaligned.	Most staff know the mission statement, and most staff actions are aligned.	All staff know the mission statement, and staff actions are aligned, with evidence of actions to support the mission statement.	Staff and parents know the mission statement, and staff actions are aligned, with evidence of actions to support the mission statement.	Staff and parents know the mission statement, and staff and parent actions are aligned, with evidence of follow-through.

Figure 9.4: Parentship mission statement continuum.

*Visit **go.SolutionTree.com/PLCbooks** for a free reproducible version of this figure.*

Use the parentship vision statement continuum shown in figure 9.5 to monitor your current building vision statement and the meaning it carries in your school community. The PST should complete this continuum each spring after receiving feedback on the parentship-perception survey.

Starting	Strengthening	Intentional	Impactful	Powerful
School staff established our parentship vision statement to describe a school that would be great to be part of and help students learn. The statement is displayed on the school website and on signs in the school.	School staff established our parentship vision statement to describe a school whose members would work collaboratively to take ownership of student learning. Staff recite the statement, and it is shared in multiple locations.	Our parentship vision statement describes how staff will commit to the fundamental purpose of the school: student learning. It is visible and present on agendas, as well as discussed in meetings. Stakeholders came to a strong consensus in crafting the statement; staff understand it must mean something.	Our parentship vision statement describes what staff want to become to fulfill the fundamental purpose of the school: learning for all students, staff, and parents. It is visible in the school and used as a mode of celebration.	Our parentship vision statement describes in detail what staff want to become to truly become the school that will ensure its fundamental purpose—ensuring learning for all students, staff, and parents—happens. It is visible and discussed in multiple settings. Everyone understands the vision and works to fulfill it.
Staff did not involve parents in the process in any way.	Staff did involve parents in the process.	Staff involved parents in the process by eliciting their feedback on the statement.	Staff involved parents in the process by eliciting their feedback on the statement. Parents were present during the vision statement's writing.	Parents are a part of the building leadership team and were integral to the writing process. Several parents provided feedback. Staff listened to parents, whose impact on the vision statement was significant.
Some staff know the vision statement, and staff actions are misaligned.	Most staff know the vision statement, and most staff actions are aligned.	All staff know the vision statement, and staff actions are aligned, with evidence of actions to support the vision statement.	Staff and parents know the vision statement, and staff actions are aligned, with evidence of actions to support the vision statement.	Staff and parents know the vision statement, and staff and parent actions are aligned, with evidence of follow-through.

Figure 9.5: Parentship vision statement continuum.

Visit **go.SolutionTree.com/PLCbooks** *for a free reproducible version of this figure.*

Author John C. Maxwell (2001) describes how high-functioning teams can improve their actions by using feedback to make changes moving forward. In his book *The 17 Indisputable Laws of Teamwork*, Maxwell (2001) describes his *law of the scoreboard*, advocating that teams make adjustments to their work only when they really know where they stand with the work. He adds that in order for teams to accomplish their goals, they must know exactly how they are doing and know if they are getting close to the goal, have achieved the goal, or did not achieve the goal (Maxwell, 2001).

Think *law of the scoreboard* when using these monitoring tools to help you in your parentship implementation.

> ## Pause and Ponder
>
> What criteria do you deem most important when using these tools to monitor your parentships' work?

Sustaining Parentships

Receiving feedback on the effectiveness of your parentships is one thing; doing something about it is quite another. This is why sustaining your effort and making improvements to your parentships are fundamental. Kanold (2011) maintains:

> What you choose to do with the results of your monitoring or *noticing*, and how you choose to use the information to influence the behavior of others, is the measure of your leadership and your discipline regarding celebration and accountability *for improved results, with consequences.* (p. 40)

In addition, author and educational consultant Douglas B. Reeves (2011) states that practices, not programs, have the greatest impact on change. For change to endure, people need to be moved to change and develop new skills and practices. People must be led, and sometimes people are messy. Developing parentships needs to become the "business we do around here" in your PLC.

> ## Pause and Ponder
>
> How can you help to continue the momentum with your parentships?

Kanold (2011) writes, "The courage to lead is forged when something personally meaningful is at stake for you and for those in your sphere of influence" (p. 40). The parentships must be something that really matters to you as a leader. The value and importance that the parentship mission and vision have within your school community also support this courage to lead. It will be difficult for you to build strong parentships without knowing exactly the impact they have on your school community, and it will be difficult for you to build strong parentships if leaders are not ready to act on the feedback they receive.

As we know, change is hard, and it can be challenging to build momentum with new initiatives and even more challenging to keep momentum over time. The Founding Associates and Consulting Partners of the Ken Blanchard Companies (2010) outline fifteen predictable reasons why change efforts typically fail:

1. People leading the change think that announcing the change is the same as implementing it.

2. People's concerns with change are not surfaced or addressed.

3. Those being asked to change are not involved in planning the change.

4. There is no compelling reason to change. The business case is not communicated.

5. A compelling vision that excites people about the future has not been developed or communicated.

6. The change leadership team does not include early adopters, resisters, or informal leaders.

7. The change is not piloted, so the organization does not learn what is needed to support the change.

8. Organizational systems and other initiatives are not aligned with the change.

9. Leaders lose focus or fail to prioritize, causing "death by 1,000 initiatives."

10. People are not enabled or encouraged to build new skills.

11. Those leading the change are not credible. They undercommunicate, give mixed messages, and do not model the behaviors the change requires.

12. Progress is not measured, and/or no one recognizes the changes that people have worked hard to make.

13. People are not held accountable for implementing the change.

14. People leading the change fail to respect the power of the culture to kill the change.

15. Possibilities and options are not explored before a specific change is chosen. (pp. 195–196)

Sustaining the Success of Your Parentships

Parentships really are the right work in a PLC. In addition to prioritizing and unwrapping standards, creating and analyzing assessments, and using intervention groups to address struggling students' learning, developing parentships to better support parents is also very important. Developing your parentships should be required work for members of a PLC.

Nine Elements for Successful Implementation

Fullan (2010a) lists these nine elements for successful implementation of initiatives.

1. A small number of ambitious goals
2. A guiding coalition at the top
3. High standards and expectations
4. Collective capacity building with a focus on instruction
5. Individual capacity building linked to instruction
6. Mobilizing the data as a strategy for improvement
7. Intervention in a nonpunitive manner
8. Being vigilant about "distractors"
9. Being transparent, relentless, and increasingly challenging

Fullan's (2010a) research provides a strong foundation for how to best sustain a change initiative over a long period of time. Each element is pivotal for positive change. Additional ways to sustain the parentship work include the following.

View the Principal as Culture Keeper

Principal leadership matters. It is imperative that the principal and building administration effectively lead the work of developing parentships and buy into the effectiveness of the work. Principals act as keepers of the culture by influencing others to fully commit to the work of parentships so that it becomes a natural part of each day—an engrained part of the building's culture.

Start With Why

The work of a PLC should always be viewed through the lens of what has the biggest positive impact on student learning. Developing your parentships is no different. To ensure buy-in from others, make sure each leader explicitly communicates that by actively supporting parents and families, the work of parentships connects to improving the educational environment and student learning.

Learn by Doing

Educators in PLCs learn by doing. They are action oriented, and they not only learn while doing the work but correct mistakes along the way to improve results. If you and your team wait until everything is perfect, you will never begin.

Reflect on Success

Another effective strategy for sustaining the work of parentships is to make *success reflection* a standing item on the agenda for PST meetings. In a PLC, actions or areas may be *tight*, meaning certain aspects of the culture are required, or *loose*, meaning educators are empowered to be more creative and innovative with their work. Your PLC should be tight when it comes to sustaining your parentships' work—that is, everyone in your school community should be required to participate. To always maintain that tight focus, make sure each meeting includes a time of reflection, in which team members can think through how they are monitoring the parentship work and attempting to sustain it. By always bringing this work to the forefront of the team, you will ensure the team maintains focus on it from month to month, day by day.

Set Aside Collaborative Time

Finding enough time to collaborate is not always easy. Hopefully you have been able to carve out the needed time to prioritize parentships. Be sure to also set aside specific time to discuss the implementation of parentships with your guiding coalition, as well as other grade-level and subject-area teams. Even if it's just once a month, this time will allow you to check whether everyone is prioritizing the work and reinforce a focus on the right work to ensure improvement.

Confront the Brutal Facts

It likely won't come as a surprise that not all team actions prove effective. Don't worry—that's normal. As Jim Collins (2001) explains, successful organizations confront the brutal facts and take an accurate, honest inventory of their current reality. You must start there. Once you do that, you can then make plans to address the lagging improvement and assess which actions are ineffective and why. Talk with others, collect feedback, make sure you have fidelity in implementation, and keep striving for improvement.

> ## Pause and Ponder
>
> What can your school do collectively to sustain the work of your parentships?

Think, Plan, and Act

Use the "Planning, Implementing, and Monitoring Tool for Sustaining the Parentships" reproducible (page 112) to bring clarity to the process of planning for and implementing new parentship initiatives. Remember to keep your focus narrow, putting your energy into one or two parentship initiatives at a time.

To use the tool, start by picking a strategy and identifying who is responsible for leading the strategy. Next, determine the resources needed, list specific action steps for successfully implementing the strategy, and think about something you can stop doing to ensure you have the time to properly focus on implementation. Finally, follow up on the success of the strategy by scanning for signs of positive impact.

Parentship-Perception Survey

Please respond to the following prompts to provide our parentship success team with valuable information on the progress of our goal of building stronger parentships in our school community.	Please indicate your response by circling a number from 1 to 5, where 1 means *strongly disagree* and 5 means *strongly agree*.				
Mission Statement					
I can state my child's school's parentship mission statement.	1	2	3	4	5
I consistently see school actions that align to the parentship mission statement.	1	2	3	4	5
I believe my child's school's fundamental purpose is high levels of student learning.	1	2	3	4	5
My child's teachers call me consistently throughout the school year.	1	2	3	4	5
If I need something, I feel confident I can contact the school and staff will provide a resource I need.	1	2	3	4	5
Vision Statement					
I can state my child's school's parentship vision statement.	1	2	3	4	5
I consistently see school actions that align to the parentship vision statement.	1	2	3	4	5
I believe my child's school is working hard to create a school to better meet my child's needs.	1	2	3	4	5
My child's school tries to involve me in important collaboration, such as volunteer opportunities, to help more students succeed.	1	2	3	4	5
My child's school often asks me for my feedback.	1	2	3	4	5
Values (Collective Commitments)					
I can state or find my child's school's parentship collective commitments.	1	2	3	4	5
I consistently see school actions that align to the parentship collective commitments.	1	2	3	4	5
I believe my child's school is working hard to commit to the promises they make about behaviors and actions we should see from them.	1	2	3	4	5
I believe my child is better able to handle failure because of actions the school and I have partnered on to help my child grow and learn.	1	2	3	4	5
I believe my child is more prepared for the future because of actions the school and I have partnered on to help my child grow and learn.	1	2	3	4	5
I believe my child has learned positive behaviors because of the modeling the school and I have provided to help my child grow and learn.	1	2	3	4	5
I am invited to be a part of school events.	1	2	3	4	5
I feel welcome when I enter my child's school.	1	2	3	4	5

Parentship-Perception-Survey Overview Tool

Number of Parent Responses (Total)	Number of Staff Responses (Total)	Celebrations	Areas of Improvement

Parentships in a PLC at Work® © 2022 Solution Tree Press • SolutionTree.com

Visit **go.SolutionTree.com/PLCbooks** to download this free reproducible.

SMART-R Goal and Timeline Tracking Template

Action Steps (What specifically needs to happen to achieve the SMART-R goal?)	Accountability (Who was responsible for implementing these actions?)	Timeline Targets (When did these actions need to be followed up on? Were they met?)	Evidence of Success (Was the goal met?)	Strengths and Weaknesses (What are the strengths and weaknesses of the goal-reaching process?)	Next Steps for Implementation (What are the next steps we will take?)
SMART-R goal to measure effectiveness of the mission statement:					
SMART-R goal to measure effectiveness of the vision statement:					
SMART-R goal to measure effectiveness of the values (collective commitments):					
SMART-R goal to measure effectiveness of student-learning strategies:					
SMART-R goal to measure effectiveness of student-attendance strategies:					
SMART-R goal to measure effectiveness of parent-attendance strategies:					

Planning, Implementing, and Monitoring Tool for Sustaining the Parentships

Strategy	Is It School or Team Based?	What Resources Are Needed?	What Action Steps Will We Take to Implement the Strategy?	What Could We Stop Doing to Make Time?	What Are the Signs of Positive Impact Following Implementation?

Epilogue: Now What?

During a leadership workshop I was facilitating at a statewide education conference, I walked around engaging with teams on leadership ideas and implementation, and I noticed one particular team having a deep conversation about the need for parents to be leaders in the school building. One member's response to a question I posed stopped me in my tracks and pretty much sums up this entire book: "It's the parents' school too." Wow! What a great response. She was right. It is the parents' school as well, and we as educators must lead our schools and our teams from that perspective.

Throughout this book, I've challenged you to reflect on how you can help lead the development of powerful collaboration between educators, parents, and students. In an article in *Voices in Urban Education*, Patricia Martinez and Joshua Wizer-Vecchi (2016) write:

> Our success depends on buy-in, leadership, and a commitment to collaboration at all levels—from the superintendent and other district leaders, to school principals, to program staff, to teachers and school staff, to parents. All of the links in this interconnected chain must work together in order for parent leadership, collaboration, and engagement to truly take hold. (p. 6)

In addition to challenging you to reflect on how to do that, I have provided numerous easy-to-use strategies that you can implement to transform and revolutionize the relationships among the educators, parents and guardians, and students in your school. I know you already have a full plate; look for actions you take that do not have the same positive leverage as improving parent partnerships, and eliminate them to make more time for parentship work. You can do this with discipline and by focusing on the right work. You are already an excellent leader, so push yourself to take that next step. It will be uncomfortable at times, but feel secure knowing that you are doing what is needed in education.

The difficulty lies not so much in developing new ideas as in escaping from old ones.

—John Maynard Keynes

This is your call to action to start this important work. Everything that has ever been done in this world started with one step, no matter how small the step. Just take the step. Ask others to take that step with you. If you wait until you have every decision figured out, you will never start. As Jim Collins and Jerry Porras (1994) exclaim in *Built to Last: Successful Habits of Visionary Companies*, "Intentions are fine and good, but it is the translation of those intentions into concrete items—mechanisms with teeth—that can make the difference between becoming a visionary . . . or forever remaining a wannabe" (p. 88).

Four Stages of Parentship Development

After you start the work, your parentships will go through four different stages. (See figure E.1 to better understand what stage your parentships are in and where you aspire to go.)

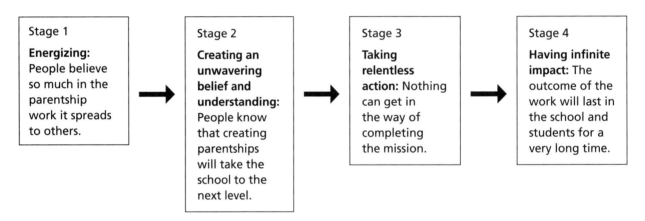

Figure E.1: The four stages of parentship development.

Stage 1: Energized People

In stage 1 of your parentships, you have a group of energized people ready to move forward. This is a great place to start. Obviously, the more the better, but you can take off with a small number. Energized people have the desire to achieve and the ability to take risks. This stage highlights the necessary ingredient of *people* in the parentship movement.

Stage 2: Unwavering Belief and Understanding

In stage 2 of your parentships, energized people can now move forward because of their unwavering belief in the work. Those with an unwavering belief truly buy in and understand the why behind the work of building your parentships because they see on a daily basis the negative effects of isolated educators, parents, and students. They see how a lack of collaboration leads to discontent, failure, and frustration among students. Those with an unwavering belief are deep thinkers, so they can navigate the path forward. This stage highlights the necessary ingredient of *knowing the work* in the parentship movement.

Stage 3: Relentless Action

In stage 3 of your parentships, energized people have developed an unwavering belief and understanding of the right work they must do. That understanding of the work needed to build the parentships has led to relentless action, in the form of regular implementation of strategies, monitoring mechanisms, and feedback loops to measure the effectiveness of this work. Those who commit to relentless action confidently take feedback to heart, making adjustments and preparing other ideations to support ways to build strong parentships. Action orientation is the key to this stage. There is no longer such a thing as good intentions; this is all about action. Schools that hesitate, or that claim they believe but don't act accordingly, are not at this stage. Only those who courageously move forward with bold actions to create powerful parent partnerships reach this stage. This stage highlights the necessary ingredient of *doing the work* in the parentship movement.

Stage 4: Infinite Impact

Schools and teams whose energized people develop an unwavering belief and understanding and do the right work—with powerful results, making the parentships a part of the fabric of each day—are now going to have an infinite impact on the school community. As you may guess, this stage is not easy to get to. One of the best indicators that you've reached this stage is when a parent can say, "It's our school too!" This stage highlights the necessary ingredient of *the collaboration with parents* in the parentship movement.

Igniting the Parentship Work

As I wrap up this book, I hope there is an urgency and fire inside you and your team to ignite the parentship work and harness the collaborative power of educators, parents, and students. It's time for parentships to transcend parent-educator relationships in education for generations to come!

References and Resources

Allensworth, E. M., Farrington, C. A., Gordon, M. F., Johnson, D. W., Klein, K., McDaniel, B., et al. (2018). *Supporting social, emotional, & academic development: Research implications for educators.* Chicago: University of Chicago Consortium on School Research. Accessed at https://consortium .uchicago.edu/sites/default/files/2019-01/Supporting%20Social%20 Emotional-Oct2018-Consortium.pdf on June 14, 2021.

American Institutes for Research. (2021, February 1). *Career and technical education: Preparing students for college and career success.* Accessed at www .air.org/resource/spotlight/career-and-technical-education-preparing-students -college-and-career-success on September 10, 2021.

Bentley, K. (2021, October 12). *Schools can maintain parent engagement with technology.* Accessed at www.govtech.com/education/k-12/schools-can -maintain-parent-engagement-with-technology on December 1, 2021.

Borba, M. (2016). *Unselfie: Why empathetic kids succeed in our all-about-me world.* New York: Touchstone.

Brown, B. (2018a). *Dare to lead: Brave work, tough conversations, whole hearts.* New York: Random House.

Brown, B. (2018b, April 19). *Design is a function of empathy* [Blog post]. Accessed at https://brenebrown.com/blog/2018/04/19/design-is-a-function-of-empathy/ on September 3, 2021.

Bryant, A. (2014, January 4). Management be nimble. *New York Times.* Accessed at https://www.nytimes.com/2014/01/05/business/management-be-nimble.html on September 7, 2021.

Carminucci, J., Hodgman, S., Rickles, J., & Garet, M. (2021, June). *Student attendance and enrollment loss in 2020–21.* Accessed at www.air.org/sites /default/files/2021-07/research-brief-covid-survey-student-attendance -june-2021_0.pdf on December 1, 2021.

Chandler, M. A. (2013, December 10). Study: Teen's knowledge of family history a sign of social-emotional health. *Washington Post*. Accessed at www.washingtonpost.com/local/education/study-teens-knowledge-of-family-history-a-sign-of-social-emotional-health/2013/12/10/72fb7606-61ce-11e3-bf45-61f69f54fc5f_story.html?wprss=rss_Copy%20of%20local-alexandria-social&utm_source=twitterfeed&utm_medium=twitter on June 14, 2021.

Chen, G. (2021, August 14). *Parental involvement is key to student success* [Blog post]. Accessed at www.publicschoolreview.com/blog/parental-involvement-is-key-to-student-success on September 6, 2021.

Cherry, K. (2021, July 26). *Characteristics and effects of uninvolved parenting*. Accessed at www.verywellmind.com/what-is-uninvolved-parenting-2794958 on December 1, 2021.

Child Trends. (2018, September 16). *Parental involvement in schools*. Accessed at www.childtrends.org/?indicators=parental-involvement-in-schools on August 31, 2021.

Coleman, P. (1998). *Parent, student and teacher collaboration: The power of three*. Thousand Oaks, CA: Corwin Press.

Collins, J. C. (2001). *Good to great: Why some companies make the leap—and others don't*. New York: HarperBusiness.

Collins, J. C., & Lazier, B. (2020). *BE [2.0]: Turning your business into an enduring great company*. New York: Portfolio.

Collins, J. C., & Porras, J. I. (1994). *Built to last: Successful habits of visionary companies*. New York: HarperBusiness.

Conzemius, A. E., & O'Neill, J. (2014). *The handbook for SMART school teams: Revitalizing best practices for collaboration* (2nd ed.). Bloomington, IN: Solution Tree Press.

Covey, S. M. R. (2006). *The speed of trust*. New York: Free Press.

DuFour, R., DuFour, R., & Eaker, R. (2008). *Revisiting Professional Learning Communities at Work: New insights for improving schools*. Bloomington, IN: Solution Tree Press.

DuFour, R., DuFour, R., Eaker, R., & Many, T. W. (2010). *Learning by doing: A handbook for Professional Learning Communities at Work* (2nd ed.). Bloomington, IN: Solution Tree Press.

DuFour, R., DuFour, R., Eaker, R., Many, T. W., & Mattos, M. (2016). *Learning by doing: A handbook for Professional Learning Communities at Work* (3rd ed.). Bloomington, IN: Solution Tree Press.

Eaker, R., & Keating, J. (2012). *Every school, every team, every classroom: District leadership for growing Professional Learning Communities at Work*. Bloomington, IN: Solution Tree Press.

Eaker, R., & Keating, J. (2015). *Kid by kid, skill by skill: Teaching in a Professional Learning Community at Work*. Bloomington, IN: Solution Tree Press.

Epstein, J. L., Sanders, M. G., Sheldon, S. B., Simon, B. S., Salinas, K. C., Jansorn, N. R., et al. (2019). *School, family, and community partnerships: Your handbook for action* (4th ed.). Thousand Oaks, CA: Corwin Press.

Fadel, C., Bialik, M., & Trilling, B. (2015). *Four-dimensional education: The competencies learners need to succeed.* Boston: Center for Curriculum Redesign.

Figner, C. (2021, April 14). *The biology behind protective "mama tiger" instincts.* Accessed at www.reviewthis.com/the-biology-behind-protective-mama-tiger -instincts on December 1, 2021.

Founding Associates and Consulting Partners of the Ken Blanchard Companies. (2010). *Leading at a higher level: Blanchard on leadership and creating high performing organizations* (Rev. and expanded ed.). Upper Saddle River, NJ: FT Press.

Fullan, M. (2010a). *All systems go: The change imperative for whole system reform.* Thousand Oaks, CA: Corwin Press.

Fullan, M. (2010b). *Motion leadership: The skinny on becoming change savvy.* Thousand Oaks, CA: Corwin Press.

Fullan, M. (2016). *The NEW meaning of educational change* (5th ed.). New York: Teachers College Press.

Gino, F. (2019, November–December). Cracking the code of sustained collaboration: Six new tools for training people to work together better. *Harvard Business Review, 97*(6), 73–81.

Gordon, J. (2018). *The power of a positive team: Proven principles and practices that make great teams great.* Hoboken, NJ: Wiley.

GreatSchools. (2011, August 11). *Why attendance matters.* Accessed at www.great schools.org/gk/articles/school-attendance-issues/#:~:text=The%20attendance %20rate%20is%20important,of%20students%20are%20frequently%20absent on June 14, 2021.

Higher Ed Dive. (2019, June 24). *Majority of primary school teachers say parents don't understand the importance of classroom, teacher engagement* [Press release]. Accessed at www.educationdive.com/press-release/20190624-majority-of -primary-school-teachers-say-parents-dont-understand-the-import/ on June 14, 2021.

Iger, R. (2019). *The ride of a lifetime: Lessons learned from 15 years as CEO of the Walt Disney Company.* New York: Random House.

Jensen, E. (2013). *Engaging students with poverty in mind: Practical strategies for raising achievement.* Alexandria, VA: Association for Supervision and Curriculum Development.

K12 Insight. (n.d.). *2019 state of K–12 customer experience report.* Accessed at www.k12cxreport.org/get-the-results/ on June 14, 2021.

Kanold, T. D. (2011). *The five disciplines of PLC leaders.* Bloomington, IN: Solution Tree Press.

Kraft, M. A., & Dougherty, S. M. (2013). The effect of teacher-family communication on student engagement: Evidence from a randomized field experiment. *Journal of Research on Educational Effectiveness, 6*(3), 199–222.

Lavalle, A. (2021). *Soon-to-be ex-teacher goes off on parents who coddle and enable kids. Internet applauds.* Accessed at www.newsbreak.com/news/2309573544 472/soon-to-be-ex-teacher-goes-off-on-parents-who-coddle-and-enable-kids -internet-applauds on December 21, 2021.

Martinez, P., & Wizer-Vecchi, J. (2016). Fostering family engagement through shared leadership in the district, schools, and community. *Voices in Urban Education, 44,* 6–13. Accessed at https://files.eric.ed.gov/fulltext/EJ1110966 .pdf on June 14, 2021.

Marzano, R. J., & Waters, T. (2009). *District leadership that works: Striking the right balance.* Bloomington, IN: Solution Tree Press.

Mattos, M., DuFour, R., DuFour, R., Eaker, R., & Many, T. W. (2016). *Concise answers to frequently asked questions about Professional Learning Communities at Work.* Bloomington, IN: Solution Tree Press.

Maxwell, J. C. (2001). *The 17 indisputable laws of teamwork: Embrace them and empower your team.* Nashville: Nelson.

Monk, J. (2018, January 31). *The importance of parent-teacher connections.* Accessed at www.socialconnectedness.org/the-importance-of-parent-teacher-connections/ on June 14, 2021.

Morin, A. (2021, January 22). *Role model the behavior you want to see from your kids.* Accessed at www.verywellfamily.com/role-model-the-behavior-you-want -to-see-from-your-kids-1094785 on December 1, 2021.

Osten, C. (2016, October 5). *Are you really listening, or just waiting to talk?* [Blog post]. Accessed at www.psychologytoday.com/us/blog/the-right-balance /201610/are-you-really-listening-or-just-waiting-talk on June 14, 2021.

Pfeffer, J., & Sutton, R. I. (2000). *The knowing-doing gap: How smart companies turn knowledge into action.* Boston: Harvard Business School Press.

Pogosyan, M. (2019, July 9). *Why we see what we want to see: The neuropsychology of motivated perception.* Accessed at www.psychologytoday.com/us/blog /between-cultures/201907/why-we-see-what-we-want-see on December 1, 2021.

PowerSchool. (2021, February 2). *Why parent engagement is important to student success* [Blog post]. Accessed at www.powerschool.com/resources/blog/why -parent-engagement-is-important-to-student-success/ on June 14, 2021.

Reeves, D. B. (2011). *Finding your leadership focus: What matters most for student results.* New York: Teachers College Press.

Roberts, M. (2020). *Shifting from me to we: How to jump-start collaboration in a PLC at Work.* Bloomington, IN: Solution Tree Press.

Satara, A. (2018, June 5). Here's why J.K. Rowling, Jeff Bezos, and Barack Obama embrace failure. *Inc.* Accessed at www.inc.com/alyssa-satara/heres-why-jk -rowling-jeff-bezos-barack-obama-embrace-failure.html on September 8, 2021.

Scamman, K. (2018, June 13). *The need for language interpretation in U.S. schools* (interactive infographic). Accessed at https://telelanguage.com/need-for -language-interpretation-in-us-schools-infographic/ on June 14, 2021.

Shellenbarger, S. (2018, August 1). Parents volunteering at school should tailor skills to different stages. *Wall Street Journal.* Accessed at www.wsj.com /articles/parents-volunteering-at-school-should-tailor-skills-to-different -stages-1533134808 on June 14, 2021.

Sheridan, S. M. (2018, August 29). *Establishing healthy parent-teacher relationships for early learning success*. Accessed at https://earlylearningnetwork.unl.edu /2018/08/29/parent-teacher-relationships/ on June 14, 2021.

Sinek, S. [simonsinek]. (2012, August 6). *A team is not a group of people who work together. A team is a group of people who trust each other* [Tweet]. Accessed at https://twitter.com/simonsinek/status/232556392114974721?lang=en on June 14, 2021.

Spiller, J., & Power, K. (2019). *Leading with intention: Eight areas for reflection and planning in your PLC at Work*. Bloomington, IN: Solution Tree Press.

Statistica. (2022). *Number of children who speak another language than English at home in the United States from 1979 to 2018*. Accessed at www.statista.com /statistics/476745/number-of-children-who-speak-another-language-than -english-at-home-in-the-us on February 10, 2022.

U.S. Department of Education. (2019, January). *Chronic absenteeism in the nation's schools: A hidden educational crisis*. Accessed at www2.ed.gov/datastory /chronicabsenteeism.html on June 14, 2021.

Waller, W. (1932). *The sociology of teaching*. New York: Wiley.

Williams, K. C., & Hierck, T. (2015). *Starting a movement: Building culture from the inside out in professional learning communities*. Bloomington, IN: Solution Tree Press.

Williams, T. T., & Sánchez, B. (2012). Parental involvement (and uninvolvement) at an inner-city high school. *Urban Education*, *47*(3), 625–652. Accessed at www.researchgate.net/publication/258198616_Parental_Involvement_and _Uninvolvement_at_an_Inner-City_High_School on June 14, 2021.

Ziglar, Z. (2019). *Goals: How to get the most out of your life*. Shippensburg, PA: Sound Wisdom.

Index

Community Connections and Your PLC at Work®
Nathaniel Provencio

In a PLC, every student, teacher, staff member, parent, and family member is vital to the operation of the school. Emphasizing transparency, mutual trust, and clarity of purpose, this resource helps create highly engaged communities collectively committed to learning for all.

BKF962

Strengthening the Connection Between School & Home (Second Edition)
Ricardo LeBlanc-Esparza and Kym LeBlanc-Esparza

Examine the pivotal role family engagement plays in student achievement with this research-based guide. Leaders will find specific strategies to involve families, including eleven ways to create a family-friendly school and advice for connecting with families who are hard to reach.

BKF486

Learning by Doing (Third Edition)
Richard DuFour, Rebecca DuFour, Robert Eaker, Thomas W. Many, and Mike Mattos

Discover how to transform your school or district into a high-performing PLC. The third edition of this comprehensive action guide offers new strategies for addressing critical PLC topics, including hiring and retaining new staff, creating team-developed common formative assessments, and more.

BKF746

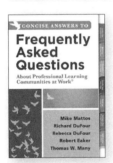

Concise Answers to Frequently Asked Questions About Professional Learning Communities at Work®
Mike Mattos, Richard DuFour, Rebecca DuFour, Robert Eaker, and Thomas W. Many

Get all of your PLC questions answered. Designed as a companion resource to *Learning by Doing: A Handbook for Professional Learning Communities at Work®* (3rd ed.), this powerful, quick-reference guidebook is a must-have for teachers and administrators working to create and sustain the PLC process.

BKF705

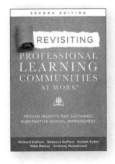

Revisiting Professional Learning Communities at Work® (Second Edition)
Richard DuFour, Rebecca DuFour, Robert Eaker, Mike Mattos, and Anthony Muhammad

Packed with research-affirmed practices, this revised classic offers a cutting-edge manifesto for PLC at Work®. The authors draw on action research and keen observation of current culture to shed new light on assessment, intervention, school culture, and other topics essential to PLC success.

BKG024

"Tremendous, tremendous, tremendous!

The speaker made me do some very deep internal reflection about the **PLC process** and the personal responsibility I have in making the school improvement process work **for ALL kids.**"

—Marc Rodriguez, teacher effectiveness coach, Denver Public Schools, Colorado

PD Services

Our experts draw from decades of research and their own experiences to bring you practical strategies for building and sustaining a high-performing PLC. You can choose from a range of customizable services, from a one-day overview to a multiyear process.

Book your PLC PD today!
888.763.9045

Solution Tree